GO
FOR
THIRD

Leadership Lessons from the
Softball Field to the Workplace

DEREK VOLK

HIGH BRIDGE
BOOKS & MEDIA

This book is dedicated to my good friend and long-time assistant coach, Tim Hannan. I miss you, Tim. (1961-2023)

CONTENTS

FOREWORD

MOST FOREWORDS TELL YOU ABOUT THE BOOK YOU'RE ABOUT TO READ, BUT this isn't most forewords, and this sure isn't like most books. So, instead of telling you about the book you're going to read, I'd rather share a personal story with you that will illustrate precisely why you should zero in on what Derek Volk has to say in his book, *Go for Third*.

My father used to use the expression "got your six" all the time. He was a fighter pilot in World War II, and when I was little, I asked him what it meant. He explained it's a military term that fighter pilots use with one another to reference their plane's rear as the six o'clock position. In other words, it's your most vulnerable position because you can't see what's behind you. It's why pilots have wingmen and travel together. If your wingman says, "I've got your six," it means, "I've got your back." When used in a team setting, business or otherwise, the expression speaks to the loyalty and cooperation you will find on a successful team. Great leaders like Derek Volk have their team members' six.

Getting someone's six is also the most powerful leadership lesson I learned during my senior year in college as a varsity lacrosse player at Fairleigh Dickinson University. After a series of injuries as a junior, I was finally healthy and was expected to be one of the best players and leaders on my team. Before I came back for my senior year, I set goals over the summer that I would be one of the leading scorers and a team captain.

One preseason practice is permanently etched in my memory. It was an early morning Saturday practice. Practice always ended with the entire team collectively having to complete dreaded sprint ladders under a prescribed amount of time. If everyone made the 200 yard cutoff time, conditioning was over. If someone didn't, *everyone* ran again until they did. (A sprint ladder, if you don't know, is a series of ten timed sprints starting at 20 yards that get 20 yards longer each time, up to 200 yards.) As you can imagine, it's easier in the beginning and gets progressively harder, especially if you're out of shape. It's even tougher if you're overweight to boot. One of our walk-on players, Jason, fit both descriptions.

A sophomore defenseman, Bill Hickey, and I were pushing each other in sprints at the end of practice. About halfway through the ladder, several of us knew, based on experience, that we were going to finish ahead of the 42-second 200-yard cutoff. So, as we were "lapping" some other players, we'd yell at them to hurry up and run faster. When Bill didn't pipe up and join us, I immediately began judging him, unimpressed.

Then an interesting thing happened. After almost everyone on the team finished the sprint ladder, Jason was still plodding away down the field. Everyone was shouting at him (some positive, some negative)—everyone except for one person. While everyone else was running their mouths, Bill went back for Jason and ran with him. He talked to him, made him laugh, and encouraged him as they finished together. Simply put, Bill had Jason's back while everyone else was talking about him behind his back … myself included.

I learned a lot about what leadership *really* was that day, much like how you're about to learn what leadership really is as you read Derek's book.

You will encounter lessons like:

- The importance of surrounding yourself with great people.

- Why mentorship matters more than you realize.

- Hiring for attitude, not just aptitude.

- Having someone's six but still leading them. (When you have someone's six, you may be located behind them, but you're still leading. You can lead by making sure others feel safe because they trust you won't let anything blindside them from behind.)

When I wasn't named one of the team captains that year, I knew exactly why. The long, hard lesson I learned was that it's more important to be the best player *for* the team than the best player *on* the team. Quite frankly, I was neither. Bill Hickey was definitely the best player for our team. Fast forward 24 years, Bill Hickey is Sergeant William Hickey of the police force in Lancaster, Pennsylvania. I share this with you because he and Derek Volk remind me a lot of one another. I'm honored to know them because they're both selfless leaders who put their people first and proudly serve their communities.

If you're reading this, then you're a member of Derek Volk's community, and I want you to know he's definitely "got your six." Derek walks his talk and is a man of high moral character. The world needs more Derek Volks because we are in an era where many leaders are more worried about covering their own six than having someone else's back.

As Derek so aptly says, surround yourself with great people. Which begs the important question:

Who's got your six in your organization?

And more importantly, who's six do you have?

That's the test of a true leader whether that's on the softball field or in the C-suite.

If you want to elevate and separate yourself from the competition, you've got the right book in your hands. Through his experience as a girls softball coach and the CEO of a highly successful company, Derek delivers a series of very compelling, powerful lessons in this book.

I promise this book will do two things for you:

It will challenge you, and it will change you.

It will challenge you to take a long hard look at the way you lead and will cause you to see things through a different lens. And that's precisely the point: In order to achieve a level of success you haven't had before, you have to be willing to lead at a higher level than you ever have before.

And if you apply Derek's timeless wisdom, it will change you. You will transform into a heart-centered leader who walks their talk and puts the organization's most valuable resource first—its people.

So, grab a highlighter, a pen, and plenty of paper to take notes. You're about to learn some incredibly valuable strategies to tangibly show your teammates and customers you've got their sixes. And in the process, you'll see that Derek has yours.

Go for third,

—**John Brubaker**
Best-selling author and professional speaker

INTRODUCTION

IN 2014, A FRIEND TOLD ME THAT I SHOULD WRITE A BUSINESS BOOK. I ASKED HIM what I should write about. He said it didn't matter—which confused me. Why wouldn't it matter what my book was about? Who would read it anyway?

He said, "Here's the deal. If you walk up to a potential customer and hand them a business book that you wrote, your credibility goes way up. It doesn't even matter if it is good. It can suck. They probably won't read it anyway. All that matters is that you wrote a business book. People think anyone who wrote a business book must know what they are talking about."

At first, it seemed ridiculous, but the more I thought about it, and remembered people handing me their business books, the more I realized his story had some logic. So, I sat down to write a business book.

As I stared at a blank computer screen, nothing came to my mind. I had nothing. And then I heard a voice, a voice that I believe was God. The voice said, "That is not the book you're supposed to write. You're supposed to write a book about Dylan." It wasn't audible, but it was as clear as anything I'd ever heard.

I began writing what became my Amazon best-selling book, *Chasing the Rabbit: A Dad's Life Raising a Son on the Spectrum*. It chronicles the experiences my wife and I had raising our son, Dylan, who is on the autism spectrum. (And now for a shameless plug—check out our website at www.chasingtherabbit.org.) Dylan and I spent five years traveling around the country speaking at autism and human resources conferences about our story. It was a wonderful experience!

Fast forward to 2021. I was out in the woods of northern Maine on a moose hunt, trying to figure out what I was going to say in an upcoming speech. I was being inducted into the Maine Manufacturer's Hall of Fame. I needed to give a speech but had no idea what to say. As I stared at the trees for hours, waiting for a moose to emerge (I did eventually get one), I came up with the idea that became this book. I titled it, "Everything I Know About Business I Learned from Coaching Girls Softball."

My credibility for writing a speech (and a book!) about softball comes from my 20 years coaching amateur girls softball, which includes 24 state and regional tournament championships. Those championships include coming in ninth in a ASA National Championship, a New England Regional Championship, and multiple Maine state and Little League championships. Besides my multiple all-star teams, I also had the honor of coaching my daughter to a D1 scholarship and dozens of girls who went on to play at the collegiate level. My records include 48–1 as a middle school coach, 56–4–1 in 2007, and 23–1–1 in 2013. Perhaps my proudest accomplishment is that I was never thrown out of a game! I absolutely loved the sport, loved the players, enjoyed every minute of my coaching experience, and miss it to this day!

With all of that to pull from, it only took me about 20 minutes to come up with more than enough content for the eight-to-ten-minute speech I was expected to give at the award ceremony. I actually had about 15 comparisons between business and coaching softball that would work for my speech. I had to narrow it down to six or seven. The speech can be seen on YouTube by searching "Everything I Need to Know about Business I Learned from Coaching Girls Softball."

When the speech was uploaded on social media, I was overwhelmed with positive responses. Quite a few people said to me, "You should write a book about that." And so, I did.

I wrote this book not with the intention of gaining more credibility, though it might do that for me with some readers, but to empower others and share leadership lessons that I have learned along the way as a business owner and as a softball coach.

We are all leaders in some way. Some of you may be business leaders, others are coaches, some run a non-profit, and many most likely lead your families. In whatever capacity you lead in your life, I hope this book gives you some real-life advice and encouragement.

God bless your journey.

Luke 12:48

—**Derek Volk**
CEO and owner of Volk Packaging Corporation and Volk Paxit
Many (many) years as a softball coach

1

GO FOR THIRD, EVEN WHEN IT'S A RISK

SOFTBALL AND BASEBALL ARE NOT THE SAME GAME. SOFTBALL IS A GAME OF speed and finesse, while baseball is a game of power. It is similar to baseball in many facets but not like baseball and its penchant for towering home runs. One big reason is the field size. As opposed to baseball fields which have 90-foot base paths, a softball field has 60-foot base paths. That 33-percent difference is critical to understanding how to coach the sport. In softball, when a player reaches first base with either zero outs or one out, it is very common for the coach to have the next batter bunt so as to move the base runner into scoring position (second or third base). I did not understand this until I had coached softball for a couple of years. And since then, I have watched too many softball games with coaches who do not understand this fundamental difference.

I always pushed my softball players to think of third base when they got to first, especially when the next batter bunted. If you assume you'll only make it to second, that's what will happen, or you'll hesitate rounding the second base bag, and that moment of apprehension will get you thrown out at third base. My players knew our goal was to go for third to force the other team to make the play. I would tell them, "Your job is to go for the extra base. If you do that, with confidence, and get thrown out at third, that's on me. I own that out. However, if you hesitate when turning for third because you are fearful of being thrown out, you own that." Robert Kennedy said, "Only those who dare to fail greatly can ever achieve greatly." I taught my players to dare to fail. I believe it is a big part of the many championships my teams won.

If you plan for average, then you'll get average, but if you plan for extraordinary, then you'll get extraordinary. How do we do that in the world of corrugated boxes? At Volk Packaging, my corrugated box manufacturing business in Biddeford, Maine, we expect every prospect to buy from us, every buyer to give us all their business, and we assume every machine we buy will be at capacity before long.

How will you plan for extraordinary in your business? Start by assuming success is yours for the taking, and force someone to stop you. Know, and write down for all to know, the characteristics of your ideal customer, and then do not be afraid to pursue them. When the buyer says, "No," consider that as just the first step in the process to get a, "Yes!" Is there something your competitor would never think to offer to a customer? Then you propose it. Think and act as if the customer is yours, every time. In the words of one of the greatest business leaders of all time, Henry Ford: "Whether you think you can or you think you can't, you're right."

Taking few risks will cause you less stress and eliminate your chance of failure, or looking like a fool, but it also destroys your ability to do something amazing. Don't live in fear. Go for third base! The worst that will happen is you'll get thrown out in a softball game, which might equate to losing a sale or opportunity in the business world. Either way, you can rest in the knowledge that you gave it your best shot, and you'll go on to fight another day. I would much rather see my player, or employee, fail while trying to do something special than sit back safely and always be average, accomplishing nothing more than getting by.

The service, quality, and the overall experience of buying from Volk Packaging is so exceptional that our attitude is, when the customer gives us a purchase order, they should thank us! That being said, I have been selling for my company for over 30 years, and no one has ever actually done that, nor do I really expect them to, but that is our mindset. We sincerely feel we are doing them a favor by providing them our boxes and services. We call the experience of buying from Volk Packaging, "Creating Excellence Together." We know our competition, and we know ourselves. I hope all my employees, particularly the sales team, know that we are better and that we offer the customer an overall experience superior to anyone else in our industry. In every interaction and in every part of the process, our employees go for third so that we can stand above the rest. If you don't believe you stand above the rest and are worth the money the customer will spend buying your product, why should they?

Proceed as if success is inevitable.

Action Plan

Where is your company acting too cautiously? Do an in-depth analysis regarding where you can take more risks. Look at where and why you are losing sales. What employees seem afraid to make decisions due to a fear of failure? What equipment or machinery do you know you need but have been too cautious about pulling the trigger on buying? Is there a person you feel confident would be a great asset to your business but have been too scared to approach? Answer those questions and then make the competitors beat you as you go for third.

2

SURROUND YOURSELF WITH GREAT PEOPLE

NO COACH CAN WIN GAMES ALONE. IN FACT, COACHES DON'T WIN GAMES AT ALL. A coach needs to have smart and hard-working people around him. Every great coach needs capable assistants, helpful parents, and, of course, high-quality players. A great coach without a great team is just a dude or lady with a clipboard, unlikely to accomplish anything truly great.

When my oldest daughter was almost nine years old, I signed her up for a clinic put on by the Scarborough High School varsity coach, Tom Griffin. Tom is arguably the best coach in the history of Maine high school softball. He started coaching softball in the early 1990s after a successful college baseball career as a pitcher for the University of Maine in Orono. The Black Bears are Maine's only D1 school, and the Maine baseball team had many successful years that included trips to Omaha, Nebraska, for the NCAA College World Series. He knew baseball but was just learning the game of softball.

It took Coach Griffin a couple of years to figure out those small differences, but once he did, he never looked back. In his first season as a high school softball coach in 1990, he won just one game. When he retired in June of 2022, Coach Griffin had amassed an amazing career. He had a record of over 500 wins and less than 100 losses with seven state championships, including a run from 2013 to 2021 without losing a single regular season game. During that stretch, he won the state title in 2013, 2017, 2018, and 2019 and likely would have in 2020 had it not be canceled because of COVID-19.

So, it was quite a compliment when Mariah was nine years old and Coach Griffin said to me, "Mariah is a good little ball player. Have you ever considered coaching travel softball?" My response, however, did not show the appreciation his question deserved.

I said, "No, never. I have a camp and a boat. I don't want to spend my summers on a softball field."

Coach Griffin's response still makes me laugh today. He looked me right in the eye and said, "Oh, it's not that big a commitment." Little did I know I'd be spending the better part of the next 15 summers on a softball field, sometimes spending as little as a week enjoying my boat and camp. But I wouldn't trade those days for anything. Coaching softball provided me with some of the best memories, friendships, and experiences of my life. To this day, when looking at the Facebook pictures of my former players becoming college graduates, wives, and moms, I feel like I have 100 nieces. And along the way, I learned a lot about running my business while coaching girls softball.

One of the first and most important lessons that I learned from Coach Griffin was to surround yourself with great people. Early in his career, Coach Griffin asked Charlie Andresen to help him with the team. Charlie's experience was also in baseball, but he raised two daughters who played softball, so he knew a few things about the game. Coach Griffin expected all of his coaches and players to walk with a high level of integrity, and Charlie did that. Their relationship required a tremendous amount of trust and faith in each other, and that's what made them such a powerhouse duo. Coach Griffin managed the team, but it was Charlie who took on the critical role of third-base coach. Softball games can easily be lost based on the decisions of the coach who is responsible for either holding the runner at third or sending her home. These decisions often lead to critical plays at the plate that can make or break a game. Coach Griffin trusted Charlie to make those calls.

In my company, I have been blessed to work with some of the most incredible, talented, smart, and hardworking people that I have ever known. Without them, I would not have accomplished much of anything. Like Coach Griffin, the ultimate decisions are mine, but every good leader needs trustworthy people of high integrity to handle the day-to-day and moment-to-moment decisions. A strong leader must have people on the field, or in the office or on the factory floor, who can take the mission, or the vision, and make it a reality. And a strong leader must trust these people to do their jobs. Anyone can hire great assistant coaches and, in business, excellent managers, but they cannot accomplish the goals you have as the leader if you micromanage everything they do. If you've surrounded yourself with great people, step back and let them be great. Walt Disney would have been just a creative artist had it not been for Roy Disney turning his dreams into realities.

During the early years of my career at Volk Packaging, I was a guy in the field. I was not leading the company; I was following the vision of my father and uncle. I spent much of that time as the company sales manager. My role at that time was to drive the company in the direction my father and uncle pointed. Thankfully for me, they trusted me like Coach Griffin trusted Charlie, so I was able to make the daily decisions that led to sales like Charlie's decisions led to runs scoring. And, like Charlie, sometimes my decisions led to outcomes opposite from what my father and uncle wanted. However, they trusted me and gave me enough leeway and freedom to make the best decision I could make at the time and then learn from it if my decision backfired.

I took that same attitude to the softball field when I became the coach. I had to because when I started coaching softball, I had no idea what I was doing. So, I brought on assistant coaches who understood the game, knew what I wanted to do during practices and games, and had the integrity to represent both the girls and me in the manner that I expected. And I let go of control and trusted them to do their jobs. Because of the people I surrounded myself with, we went on to have great success as a team!

Action Plan

Do an extensive assessment, get outside help—if needed—from your team, and begin looking for people to fill in any leadership gaps you might have in your organization. Do you have a company-wide organizational chart with not only who is currently at the company but open positions that need to be filled now or in the future? Sit with your leadership team or an advisor to review your organizational chart. Make sure you have clearly written job descriptions for every box on the organizational chart. From this work, you will be able to determine if you need to expand your team and if the team you do have is in the right seats. As Gino Wickman says in the book *Traction*, make sure the right people are in the right seats.

3

CONSIDER THE ADVICE OF YOUR COACHES

THERE ARE VERY FEW LEADERS, IF ANY, WITH THE ABILITY TO RISE TO GREAT success if they only listen to their own advice. Quite the opposite is true actually. Many come to ruin when they start ignoring the advice of the capable and trusted advisors they have surrounded themselves with.

Not until Napoleon Boneparte stopped listening to his generals did his army face devastating losses. In 1812, headed into the winter months, Napoleon invaded Russia despite the fact that his generals suggested they prepare their soldiers for a later attack in the warmer months. The French invasion of Russia led to the death of hundreds of thousands of Napolean's troops. As many as 100,000 died, not from combat but from the frigid weather. As foolish as we now know Napoleon's strategy was, we can learn from his mistakes. Whether you are running a small business, a softball team, or an army, you must listen to your advisors. The surest way to failure is to think you alone have all the answers.

Watch the final out of a big baseball game or the final seconds of a basketball or football game, and you'll see that the first thing the winning coach will do is high five or hug his coaching staff. A good leader knows that although he may love every one of his ideas, some of them suck. You need to be willing to listen to the people you have on your team and trust that sometimes, even if your name is on the building or your shirt says "Head Coach," you don't have a monopoly on good ideas. What's the point of surrounding yourself with great people if you don't heed their words? You have to listen to their advice, and often that requires putting your ego aside to accept when sometimes they have a better plan than you do.

I knew very little about the game of softball when I first started coaching. I coached a couple of years of a youth league when I was in college, but it was not a serious league, and the girls, although wonderful to work with, were not serious about the sport. It was simply a summer activity their parents signed them up for to keep them active until school started again. And not so luckily for them, they got a college kid who never played baseball past Little League as their coach. I didn't really understand the game of softball. So, I studied what the elite players and coaches said, and I listened to people around me who knew more than I did. As I advanced my coaching to Little League, all-star teams, middle school, and high-level travel softball, it became more and more evident that I needed good assistant coaches.

When I needed to hire an executive assistant at Volk Packaging, I had certain criteria in mind. One of those was hiring someone who did not tell me everything I said or did was great. When it came down to the final two candidates, the question that got one hired and one shown the door was, "What will you do if I bring you an idea that is just stupid and you know it is never going to go well?"

One candidate replied, "Well, you're my boss, so if you think it is a good idea, I'd support it as best I can."

The second candidate said, "I'd probably hear you out, go back to my office to consider my position, and then I'd come back a couple of hours later to ask if you had considered all the options and the possibilities. I would try to help you see that maybe it wasn't such a good idea." I hired the second candidate, and she did a terrific job helping me see my ideas from a different perspective.

Many years ago, we had a very outdated computer system that was used to manage our pricing. My vice president of operations, Mike Rousselle, who had been with the company for 30 years, had an idea to change the way we price boxes that are parts of a set—for example, an open-top box with a cover or a box with partitions inside. I hated his new idea because I was very comfortable with what we had been doing. At one meeting, when we were debating the merits of both options, Mike said, "Hey, look, you're the boss, so if you tell me we have to do it the old way, then we'll go back to doing it that way."

I thought about it for a moment and then said, "Okay, go back to the old way."

Mike looked me right in the eye and said, "We're not doing that. My way is better."

I jokingly said, "Whose name is on the building again? Why did you ask me that question if you had no intention to change?"

He said, "I didn't think you'd call my bluff."

I had a tremendous amount of respect for Mike, so I agreed to try it his way. It was hard to adjust the way I did pricing, but Mike was 100 percent correct. His idea was better, much better. And because of his "suggestion," the company was better, too.

I have been very blessed to also have a leadership team consisting of my plant manager, customer service manager, designer, sales manager, CFO, COO and CHRO who are not shy to share their opinions with me. I never want to be surrounded by yes-men. In the words of Margaret Thatcher, "If two people always agree, one of them is unnecessary." Make sure no one on your team is unnecessary by inviting and encouraging input and advice from your business' "coaches."

Action Plan

Sit down with your "coaches" and ask for honest opinions about how things are working at your organization and what could be improved. And actually listen to them. I will warn you that this can be difficult. They may tell you things that you don't want to hear. Do not interrupt them with excuses or logical explanations. Your instinct may be to get defensive. Try not to. The suggestions they may make could be about systems or processes that you created. As sales guru David Sandler says, "No one wants to hear that their kid is ugly." What you created may not be best for the organization. I encourage you to hear them out because what you wish you could close your eyes and ears to is often what you need to see and hear the most.

4

PEOPLE PERFORM BETTER WHEN THEY FEEL GOOD ABOUT THEMSELVES

AT A SOFTBALL CONVENTION I ATTENDED MANY YEARS AGO, THE 11-TIME NA-tional champion and winningest softball coach in D1 history said, "Boys feel good when they play good. Girls play good when they feel good." Although her grammar wasn't perfect, the sentiment is, and it also holds true in the business world, and not just for women. If the people working for you feel good about themselves, and they feel like they are a contributing factor to the team's success, they will perform better. Yell, scream, and put people down, and you will find the results your company achieves are greatly diminished.

I am not, by nature, a yeller. The idea of screaming at people to get them to do what I want just never seemed to make much sense to me. It's not the way my natural leadership manifests. I know there are legendary leaders like Vince Lombardi, General George C. Patton, and Bill Parcells who did that with great success, but I'm not like them. If you find that you get your best results by yelling and screaming at people, you might want to skip this chapter. To me, that is not leadership. That is bringing people where you want them but under duress or even direct threat. I understand there can be a place for that (for example, in the military where you're in life-and-death situations), but I don't feel that is an effective way to run a privately held business or a softball team.

President and Five Star General Dwight D. Eisenhower, who led us to victory in World War II, had a simple way of explaining leadership. He laid a piece of string on a table and said, "Pull the string, and it will follow you wherever you go. Push it, and it will go nowhere at all. It's just that way when it comes to leading people."

Back in 2007, I had one of the most talented groups of young girl softball players that I would ever have the opportunity to coach. In fact, 11 of the 13 girls on that team went on to play at some level of college softball. (My daughter, Mariah, could also have been playing college softball at the D3 school that she attended. However, she decided that that was not what she wanted to do so that would've been 12 out of 13.) During that 2007 season, I had a player on my team whose mom was very serious about softball, maybe a bit too serious. Afterall, they were only 11- and 12-year-old girls. In July of that summer, we won the regional championship which qualified us for a national competition. We were practicing every day in preparation to attend the ASA national championship in early August.

One day that July, I received an email from the helicopter mom. Her email informed me that she did not feel I was "intense enough" to prepare the girls to attend the national competition. One of the rules I always had while coaching, and could certainly be replicated in the business world, was not to reply to any email from a parent. There are a number of reasons why I had that rule, but one of the most obvious reasons is that it is always less ideal to reply to someone who is upset with you by email. Without tone, pitch, and body language, you will never know how your email is interpreted. Scientists have determined that only 7 percent of communication is the actual words that are used in an interaction. As much as 93 percent of communication resides outside the words. It is that tone, pitch, facial expressions, and overall nonverbal communication that makes up the bulk of human interactions. Given that fact, it can be very dangerous to reply to upset coaches, parents, or anyone in the workplace—an upset customer, coworker, or employee. When I received that email from this mom, my response was brief and direct. I simply emailed back, "Thanks for your feedback. Let's talk after practice tonight."

She came to almost every practice, often sitting in a chair or standing behind home plate coaching her daughter. That is not a situation any coach wants to deal with. Thankfully, she did it in a relatively caring, respectful, and harmless manner which is why I never asked her to stop. She would not contradict anything I said but rather would encourage her daughter, so I didn't have a huge problem with it. Before I saw her that night, I worked through, in my head, what I would say to her after practice. When practice ended and all the girls had packed up to go, I approached her. I started with a question: "Can you tell me a little bit more about the concerns that you expressed via email?"

She said that she did not feel like I was intense enough to get the girls ready for the competition in August. She said there was "too much laughing and giggling going on during the practices." I listened to her concerns and then I addressed them as best I could, and with respect. I reminded her that these were 11- and 12-year-old girls. I also told her that when the games begin, they will play harder for each other if they truly care about each other than they ever would for me. I said, "If you watch them during the drills, they are extremely focused and perform at a very high level of play. That's what got us the regional championship win, and that's what will help us be successful when we get to the nationals. I want them to laugh and to giggle. If they're not having fun, they won't perform. As long as they're focused when it matters, I'll take all the laughing and giggling that they have inside them because it bonds them."

Now, despite my efforts trying to explain my coaching philosophy to this particular mom, I'm not sure I made much progress. However, she didn't bring it up again, so I considered that a success. And when we came in ninth at that national competition, competing against girls from all over the country, she had even less to say.

The same thing can be said about your coworkers and your employees. Yes, they work for you. Yes, you may be the one who signs the front of their paychecks. But if they don't like their coworkers and if they don't care about doing well both for themselves and their peers, all your paychecks in the world are not going to keep them in your organization. And just a paycheck from you is certainly not going to get them to perform at the highest levels that they're capable of. They will do exceptional work only if they feel good about themselves and care about you and the people that they work with every day.

Action Plan

Make a commitment to tell someone in your organization that you appreciate them. Be specific in your encouragement and compliments to them. Then, do it again with someone else the next day. And keep doing it.

5

SMALL BALL MATTERS

SMALL BALL IS A TERM USED TO DESCRIBE CERTAIN TYPES OF PLAY IN BOTH baseball and softball. Small ball includes strategies such as bunting, stealing, drawing walks, and other tactics of the game that are not just about waiting for the next big hit to win a game. What often makes the headlines are home runs or no-hitters, but games are often won on a bunt or a timely stolen base (i.e., Dave Roberts circa 2004). When my daughter Lilly was in the Little League District Championship in 2010, we were tied 0–0 in the sixth inning. As we went to bat in the top of the last inning, I said to the girls, "We're going to win this game. And you know how we are going to win? We are better bunters, and we are better base runners. We are going to find a way to get a runner on base, and then we are going to play small ball until someone scores." We scored three runs and then shut them down in the bottom of the inning to win the championship.

Like home runs and no-hitters, big bonuses, raises, and awards are wonderful. I don't think anyone could argue with that fact. But the text wishing someone well if they are out sick, the handwritten birthday card, or the hat you bought the Broncos fan on your business trip to Denver can often make a bigger impact than a bonus or promotion. The cliché is so true: "People don't care how much you know until they know how much your care." While this saying is old and possibly tired, it is still true. I never saw my players as just girls I was coaching. I always saw them as young people whom I could impact deeply, depending on how much I could build a relationship with them.

Knowing what is important to your players (and your employees) makes a huge difference to them. When I was a softball coach, I always got to know them beyond how well they performed on the ball field. What were their hobbies? Who were their best friends? What other sports did they play? Which classes were they struggling with or excelling at? What music did they like? These questions all seem very superficial, but they were important to my players, and these types of questions will be very important to your employees. Find out what is important to them, not only professionally but personally. Learn about their kids (everyone's favorite topic). Know who their significant other is. Do they like to hunt or fish? What sports teams do they root for? What do they look forward to doing on weekends? If you can discover what matters to your employees, you can customize how you reward them, thank them, and encourage them. Additionally, you will build a relationship with them, and if you build a relationship with them, you can push them harder, expect more from them, and develop real trust between you and them.

I took this practice of learning about people from the field into my business. In 2019, my uncle retired from our family business, leaving me as the sole owner. This was an opportunity for Volk Packaging to become truly mine. As I thought about that exciting and overwhelming responsibility, it occurred to me that even after almost 30 years running and working in my family business, there was a lot I could learn. I knew that my knowledge of the business was strong, but, like the little things I do for other people outside my business, I figured that there were probably little things that I could do to learn more about my company and the people who have made it successful for so many years. I created something that I called "Breaking Bread with Derek." I set a goal in 2019 to have breakfast, lunch, or dinner with every single employee. I wanted to know from them what was going well and what was not going well. I also wanted to learn more about my company from the ground level employee all the way to the highest levels of the leadership team. I created a little form (See the appendix) for people to fill out so it would help us get a conversation going.

It didn't take long before I realized what a great idea this was. As you might expect, some of the meals were awkward at first because I didn't really know the employee at all. Some of the meals were awkward because I knew the employee as a coworker (in some cases, for most of my life), but I had never sat down and had a meal with them. The discomfort often went both ways. Many people are hesitant about meeting with the boss one-on-one, much less outside of work. I tried to quickly ease their reluctance to talk by asking about their family, kids, and hobbies. If you get people talking about what they love, conversations flow much better. It doesn't sound like much, but people told me things about my company that I had no idea about, and I not only learned so much about the business, but I also learned about my employees as individuals. I even had one employee, who had been with the company for over 25 years, say to me, "I don't mean to insult you, but how much do you know about what happens in the plant?"

I said, "Well, I think I have a pretty good handle on what happens out there, but I'm sure there are a lot of things that I am unaware of. Why do you ask?"

He said, "I would like to give you a tour of your company if you don't mind. I'd like to show you all the things that we've done over the years that you may or may not be aware of. Things that have made your company better."

I told him I loved that idea. We ended up having dinner for almost three hours, talking about the company and our lives, and I got to know him at a level that, in 25 years of working together, we had never reached before. A few weeks later, he gave me that tour. Some of the things he showed me I was aware of, but a lot of them I was completely clueless about. It was a terrific way for him to share his pride in the company that we had built together over so many years.

I learned one very interesting thing while doing "Breaking Breads:" People will tell you things over a meal that they would never tell you when you're just walking through the plant or in an office setting. There is something about sitting down to have a meal with somebody that changes the dynamic of the relationship. These meals were not formal. I didn't have an agenda or take notes. They were essentially an act of verbal small ball. Light and personal conversations in an effort to get to know my coworkers better so, as their boss, I could serve them more effectively. I am convinced that true leadership is more about serving than it is about giving orders.

I completed my goal in 2019, but then in early 2020, we were all shut down by COVID. While my business was considered essential, so we never closed for a single day, all the restaurants were closed. My Breaking Bread meals had to take a hiatus. I was very disappointed because I felt like I gained so much from those conversations. As soon as things opened up again, I started coordinating Breaking Breads again. And I still do them to this day.

Playing small ball in your business applies to more than just your employees. Doing the little things makes a difference to everyone you come in contact with. I often send notes, magazine articles, newspaper stories, or anything else that I can think of to customers who would appreciate the gesture. It is, or can be, time-consuming to do this on an ongoing basis, but the reward is well worth the investment of time. I hardly ever read a newspaper or even my hunting magazines or *Sports Illustrated* without somewhere in my mind thinking, *I must know someone who would appreciate reading this.* When those names come to my mind, I bring the article to work, make photocopies, and start mailing them out. The interesting thing about doing things like this is I get little to no feedback whatsoever. Very rarely does anybody thank me, but that's not the objective. The reward is not in receiving a thank you. If you do it just to receive praise, you are totally missing the point. The value comes in knowing you may have brightened someone's day, even if just for a few minutes. Take pleasure in that. And, of course, the long-term objective is slow and steady relationship building. Hopefully, by letting a customer or employee, or even a friend or family member, know that you are thinking of them beyond just the opportunity to sell them some boxes or personal gain, you are building trust and strengthening that relationship.

I want my employees and my customers to know that I care about them. I don't just care about them putting in a full day's work, and I don't just care about my customers placing orders—I care about them as people, and I find joy in sharing what I think they might be interested in. That's how I play small ball in my business. Another perfect example of that was when one of my office workers sent an email telling everybody that her daughter was selling magazine subscriptions. I subscribed to a couple of magazines that were of interest to me. But then, as I went through the list of magazines offered, I realized how many of my employees would enjoy some of these magazine subscriptions.

When all was said and done, I spent over $1,000 on magazine subscriptions for my employees. Several months went by, and those magazine subscriptions were surely arriving at their homes, and yet only one employee sent me a text with a photo of the magazine asking if I ordered a subscription for them. I didn't tell anybody that I did this. To be honest, I thought they would probably figure it out. But if they didn't, well, that was fine, too. I know the magazines that arrived made my employees happy. At the end of the day, that was worth the effort and the money.

Of all the chapters in this book, this one about playing small ball is probably my favorite. I think it's my favorite because, frankly, I'm really good at it. And I enjoy doing it. It gives me pleasure to make someone happy. I give my father credit. He is a wonderful role model when it comes to small ball. He is still, at 85 and retired in Florida, the first person to call an employee who is sick or lost a loved one. He is the master of small ball because he truly cares about people. If that isn't the case with you, you might want to think twice about your role as a leader. Why? Because doing things for others and helping others become successful, make money, and be all they can be are essential for true servant leadership. If this is not a natural instinct for you, my suggestion is you fake it until you make it. I promise you it will pay dividends beyond what you can imagine. And who knows, maybe you'll find you like it more than you think.

The most important part of this advice is to actually care because, trust me, you can fake it for a while, but in time, people know when you are not sincere. People, namely your employees and your customers, want to know you care about them as an actual person, not just as a tool toward your success. Knowing this helps build relationships which creates happier employees and satisfied customers. Small ball matters.

Action Plan

Start a list of what is personally important to the people in your organization, your customers, and your vendors. Begin to look for ways to thank people based on their interests.

6

KEEP YOUR EYE ON THE BALL

KEEPING YOUR EYE ON THE BALL IS PRETTY OBVIOUS. OR, IN THE WORDS OF BILL
Belichick, "Do your job." Know what you do. Stay focused. Do it as
best you can. If you start looking around the stands for who is watching you, they won't be impressed with what they see.

This principle of keeping your eye on the ball is as relevant in business
as it is in softball. It is critical that leaders of business stay focused on what
they do well as a leader and as an organization. I cannot say that I haven't
had times in my career where I've taken my eye off the ball. Sometimes
allowing my gaze to stray comes from pure exhaustion, and sometimes it
comes from boredom. However, keeping your eye on the ball and staying
focused on what you do well will give you your best chance for success.
Currently, with constantly changing technology and opportunities for get-
rich-quick schemes all over social media, staying focused on what you do
well is vital.

Keeping your eye on the ball is even more important if it is your company. If you have skin in the game or, as many business owners do, if you
have your personal home on the line, you have no option but to keep your
eye on the ball. Any deviation or distraction could be devastating. When
you own a company, when it's your name on the front of the paychecks,
keeping your eye on the ball is the only option. If you strike out because
you got distracted by some shiny object that grabs your attention, you
could be putting your house and all the people who count on you in peril.

I remember a conversation that I had with my daughter when she was
13 years old. My wife and I were sitting at the dinner table with her, my
youngest. I was telling them that there was a rumor going around my company that we were for sale. At the time, I had no intention to sell the

company, so I called a company meeting to explain to everybody that I didn't know where the rumor came from, but it was not true. After I got done telling the story, my daughter looked up at me and said, "I thought I was taking over the company someday."

I'm not sure what my face looked like, but I assume my jaw was close to the table. I had never heard her say anything like that before. None of my kids had ever expressed interest in joining our family business. My 13-year-old daughter blurting that out during dinner was quite a surprise. I asked her where that comment came from. She said, "Well, it seems like a really nice place to work, everybody's nice, you make a good living, and nobody else seems to want it." I thought for a moment about her comments before replying. This was a big moment for me. I wanted to do what my father had always done very well.

I always knew my father wanted me, as well as my brother and sister, to join the family business. While I knew that was his desire, he never pressured me to do so. There is a very fine line to walk in getting a family business successfully transitioned to the next generation. It is a delicate walk between encouraging and pressuring. I have to give my father a lot of credit for always encouraging me but never pressuring me.

I said to my daughter, "Yes, it is a nice place to work, and yes, there are very nice people there. And you can make a nice living. However, taking over the family business because nobody else wants to do it is the absolute worst reason to do it. This is not a job. It's a life. There's no off switch. There's no punching out. The business is always on your mind. If you want to join the family business, you can decide that when you're older. You're 13, and there's no hurry, but you can't do it just because nobody else is doing it because it just won't work." She listened and, to my disappointment, has never mentioned it again. What I was saying to her, essentially, is that when running a family business or being the leader of any organization, whether it's a business or a nonprofit or a team, you have to always keep your eye on the ball.

We took our eyes off the ball for a while in the early 1980s, and it cost us a lot of money and wasted time. We are located in Maine where there is a thriving seafood industry. In the early 1980s, we began selling a seafood box that included a Styrofoam tub and gel ice packs. This was a big departure from our long and successful history of just selling corrugated. We made an assumption that if we found a better tub and improved ice packs, the consumers of seafood boxes would buy it. We never actually asked any of them. Our assumption was wrong. The fishermen at the time just wanted the least expensive product. The exceptional quality of our tubs and ice and the hefty price that went along with them were not appealing to them. We took our eyes off the corrugated ball, got distracted, and it was a big bust.

Action Plan

Take an honest assessment of what is distracting you and then make a plan to eliminate the distractions so you can focus better on what is most important.

7

TRUST IS EVERYTHING

AS A COACH OR AS A LEADER IN YOUR COMPANY, YOU MOST LIKELY WANT TO have your hands in everything, but that is impossible. Whether on the field or at work, no one can be everywhere at all times. And if you try to be everywhere always, you'll most likely be labeled a "micromanager," and you will drive your players or employees crazy. Not only that, but you will drive yourself crazy because if you are watching over everything and doing all the work, how will you ever have time to take vacations and enjoy life outside of work? You cannot be a one-person show. It is bad for your organization and unhealthy for you as a person.

So how do you keep yourself from becoming a micromanager and ensure long-term success? One of the best strategies is to get your players to work together. And the best way to get them to work together is to have them trust each other. When I was coaching, I would frequently create drills that required the players to not only lead the drill but also do the scoring. If it was a contest, I made sure that they were watching out for their teammates and helping them improve their game.

Trust is even more important in a work environment. There are so many times when you, as the boss, want to just give an answer. Somebody brings you a problem, and you provide a solution. Many times, those situations occur because there is a conflict between two employees. Please understand that when I say conflict, I don't necessarily mean negative conflict. It could just be a disagreement among friends. It could be that they both agree on the end goal, but they just see different ways of going about a certain task or problem-solving activity. Of course, if the conflict involves mistreatment or destructive behavior, you will have no choice but to use your authority to properly address the situation. Abuse can never be tolerated or negotiated. Assuming we are not talking about abuse or harassment, by allowing the team to work together to arrive at a solution, you are inherently creating trust between them.

As a history buff, I read a lot of books about war. One theme that runs through every single book or movie about war is why they do what they do. And that consistent theme is not patriotism, love of country, duty, or even courage. The recurring narrative is that their heroism was done for the men to their left and to their right. Their band of brothers. And nothing creates that bond more than trusting that they have each other's backs. As John Brubaker eloquently wrote in the foreword, they have each other's six.

Trust is everything between team members, and it is everything when it comes to a leader and the team. It is important for your team to trust you as a leader, but it is also critically important that they trust each other for those days, hours, or even moments when you are not there to make a decision. They must trust that the person next to them can not only make a wise decision but can make a wise decision that's good for the whole team, not just their own self-interest. Trust creates a team atmosphere, and a team working together will almost always outperform a person trying to accomplish something on his or her own. There is a reason that the cliché saying "strength in numbers" exists. There is definitely strength in numbers, but without trust, it is more accurately "chaos in numbers."

Perhaps the greatest leader when it comes to creating trust was Walt Disney. At Disneyland and Disney World, the employees, known as cast members, all have the authority to make virtually any decision that they feel is necessary to ensure that the customers, affectionately known as visitors, are happy. If a visitor is upset or unhappy, it is incumbent on all cast members to take action, regardless of cost, to make the visitor happy again. Without that ability and the trust that Disney gives all its cast members, it would be a lot more difficult to call it "the happiest place on Earth."

I once read an amazing story about how far Disney goes to accomplish their mission. A little boy was crying, upset because, after he waited over an hour in the hot Florida sun, Peter Pan left the autograph line just as the little boy was about to reach the front of the line. A cast member, who was sweeping the sidewalk, saw the sad little boy leaving the Magic Kingdom. He asked the boy why he was crying, and the parents explained that he did not get Peter Pan's autograph. The cast member asked for his name and where he was staying.

An hour or so later, when the family arrived back in their room, they were shocked to see a stuffed Peter Pan on the bed with a note that said, "I'm sorry I missed you today. I hope this autograph brings a smile to your face." This cast member felt so empowered by his employer's trust in him that he made this little boy's day. That is what I call putting trust in your employee, and it would be hard to argue that that is anything short of exceptional customer service! If you want your players and employees to trust you, trust them first. When you model trust between you and your team members and give them the opportunity to count on each other, they will instinctively develop trust between themselves.

Action Plan

Think about some decisions that you always make for your team. The next time the decision needs to be made, allow them to make it without you. And here is the hardest part: Let it be the final decision. If you let them make decisions and then overrule them, you will find the goal to build trust disappears quickly.

8

WHEN YOU KNOW THERE ARE LIMITED RESULTS, PREPARE FOR ACTION.

HERE IS A SITUATION IN A SOFTBALL GAME THAT COACHES CALL A 3–2–2. IT occurs when there is a runner on either first base, first and second base, or the bases are loaded with two outs and a full count (three balls, two strikes). In this scenario, there are only a limited number of outcomes. One, the batter could strike out, thus ending the inning. Two, the batter could walk which would either keep a force (the fielder only has to step on the next bag to get a runner out—they do not have to tag anyone with the ball) or, if the bases are loaded, drive in a run. Third, the runner could ground out or fly out, thus ending the inning. Lastly, and ideally, the batter gets a hit, and the runners advance, possibly even scoring. Those are the only outcomes. Therefore, in a 3–2–2 situation, all the runners take off for the next bag as soon as the ball is out of the pitcher's hand. There is no downside to this move because the batter either gets a hit, hits into an out, strikes out, or walks, so the runners may as well be on the go.

The most important part of this situation is making sure the runners, especially the younger ones, understand what is about to happen and why it is happening. The coach should not only direct all the players on the bases to run on the release of the ball, but they also need to explain why they are doing it so that, in time, they perform the play instinctively. Learning to play instinctively helps increase their skill level.

I learned a fascinating theory about skill levels when someone taught me the four levels of consciousness. It revolutionized my training and coaching from that day forward. The same four levels apply to softball, other sports, new jobs or unfamiliar tasks, and virtually anything we learn that is new to us. Stage 1 is when you are unconsciously incompetent. This is the point where you don't even know what you don't know. A U10 (U10 means a player who is on a team that is for girls 10 and under. U12 would be for girls 12 and under, and so forth for U14, U16, etc.) softball player does not understand that she must run on release (when the pitcher lets go of the ball) in a 3–2–2 situation, and even if you were the first base coach who told them to run, she would have no clue why she is doing it. She is unconsciously incompetent. She doesn't even know what she doesn't know.

Stage 2 is when you become consciously incompetent. When you get to Stage 2, you are still incompetent. "Incompetent" is not used as an insult. It simply means you cannot perform tasks without being told. You know there are things you need to learn about the game or job to become a better teammate. You are aware of your shortcomings.

When you get to Stage 3, you are consciously competent. Players in Stage 3 are usually a U12 or even U14 player. Rarely did I coach a girl who was consciously competent at nine or 10 years old. When someone is consciously competent, they know what they need to do, they know how to perform and how to play the game (be it softball, sales, or whatever your hobby or vocation is), but they must think about it. This player, in a 3–2–2 situation on the softball field, will think to herself, *Okay, I am at first. There is a girl at the plate with a full count, and we have two outs. I need to run when the pitcher releases the ball.* That is being consciously competent.

The ultimate goal of any softball coach, player, employee, or business owner is to get to Stage 4. At Stage 4, you are unconsciously competent. When that runner is at first base and the count goes to three balls and two strikes with two outs, she doesn't have to think at all—she just runs when the ball comes out of the pitcher's hand and flies toward the next base. No thinking is required, as instinct and years of training have kicked in. The player is 100 percent prepared for that 3–2–2, and if the first base coach reminds her to run on release, she thinks to herself, *Yeah, obviously. It is 3–2–2.*

When I began my career in management, I was a 26-year-old sales manager. Everyone on my team was at least 10 years older than I was. That difference doesn't seem like much now that I am 54 and they are in their early to mid-60s, but when I was 26 and they were 35 or older, it was quite intimidating. At my first sales meeting, I informed them that we would be doing role plays. As I recall this first meeting, over 25 years later, I can almost hear the complaining and see the eyes rolling. No one wanted to do role plays because no one wanted to look stupid or unskilled in front of their peers. I told them that I understood that the idea made them uncomfortable, but this was no different from a team practicing before a game. I asked, "Would you rather make mistakes in front of these people who all care about you and want to help you or would you rather make them in front of a customer and potentially lose a sale?"

I knew it was just fear and awkwardness when some of them replied, "In front of a customer!" I then explained that, when it came to sales, my goal was for them to become unconsciously competent in *all* sales scenarios. I wanted to role play the real-life situations they were facing so no matter what a customer threw at them, they would be prepared without having to think about the answer.

One of the biggest mistakes businesspeople make is not listening well enough to the customer. The reason this happens so often is because they are not well prepared to face difficult situations. They are not at Stage 4 yet. As they sense a challenge while the customer is still talking, they are frantically preparing their response. This does not happen to the unconsciously competent salesperson. That salesperson is so well trained and so prepared that he or she can remain relaxed and listening before responding to anything thrown their way. There is no moment of panic when they think, *Oh my goodness, now that she said that, what do I say when she is done talking?* Someone who is unconsciously competent can just listen because they are prepared for anything, even a 3–2–2 situation.

Action Plan

What situations do you get in that cause you to have to think about a response? Practice them. Role-play them with someone you trust. Get yourself totally ready for your 3–2–2 situation so you are always ready to run!

9

TIME MATTERS

WE LIVE IN A WORLD OF INSTANT GRATIFICATION. PEOPLE WANT RESULTS, and they very rarely have the patience to wait for them. Unfortunately, the reality for softball players and employees and everybody in between is that positive results often take time. When coaching, there is no substitute for time. Knowing how to hit a 60-mile-per-hour fastball or play the field properly is the result of repetitious actions performed over and over again for years. We begin when girls are very young, as little as five or six, teaching them the fundamentals of the game, how to correctly stand at the plate, choose the right pitch, bend their knees, rotate their hips, drive their hands through the ball, and extend the follow-through for maximum power. We teach our players the skills and then have them perform the motions again and again until they can do so unconsciously. They need to become unconsciously competent, as we discussed in the previous chapter. The same is true in the workplace.

When I was a young sales manager, after spending several years in various parts of the company, I hired some new salespeople. The first thing I did was put them in the factory. My thought was, *I want them to understand the process of making a box immediately, and then I'll let them out on the road to sell.* However, as time passed, those sales representatives were kind enough to be honest with me, and they told me how useless that plan was. I sent them into an environment without context. What was the point of seeing boxes run through a machine before understanding how those boxes would be used by a customer or why one style, design, or strength of a box was better than another? They were unconsciously incompetent, and I was wasting their time. I learned that, before they went into the factory, they needed an understanding of what customers want and need when choosing a box or a box company. They needed to understand what questions to ask and what the purpose of being in the factory was for them. They needed to be consciously incompetent. They had to know what they didn't know so they could seek the answers.

Instead of sending them straight into our factory to watch machines run with no understanding of what it meant to their job, they hit the road and began talking to customers to gain a fuller understanding of what happens in the factory to produce the boxes. I then spent several months training them in the sales skills required and how to use those skills to service their customers. What is the objective of the customer's box? What would they be shipping? How much did it weigh, and was it breakable? And, of course, what were they willing to pay us for the box and the service Volk Packaging provided? As they gained these skills, the salesperson became consciously competent. He or she could do the job but had to think about what they were doing. When the customer said X, the salesperson had to think, *Okay, what am I supposed to say to that?* This is probably the longest stage in the competency process. It can last for years, but like learning to pitch or hit a fastball, eventually, you can do it without even thinking. Once they understood how the customer was impacted by the boxes we sold them, I would have them spend time in the factory. This way they knew what questions to ask and how they could use that knowledge to better service their customers.

Competitive athletes and energetic, enthusiastic employees are not always patient when they have to spend time training, but nothing could be more critical to their long-term success. Only through rigorous preparation will the employee or player become unconsciously competent. No matter what the customer says or what ball gets hit or thrown toward them, they immediately respond because they have practiced it so many times. They don't have to even think. They say practice makes perfect, but that's a myth. There was only one person who was ever perfect. Practice actually makes permanent and consistent. The rest of us, with enough time and practice, can become unconsciously competent. And that should be the goal of every athlete and employee.

Action Plan

At my monthly company meetings, I always have a "Question of the Month." I ask questions that challenge the employees and myself to make the company better by making us all a little better. One month I asked, "What skills are you lacking that would make you enjoy your job more and feel greater accomplishment at the end of a day at Volk Packaging?" The results were excellent. We signed some people up for classes, did some one-on-one work with others, and helped cross-train some others. The employees and the company were better once we learned where we had some skills gaps.

10

ADMIT WHEN YOU SCREWED UP

IN HIS BEST-SELLING BOOK, *EXTREME OWNERSHIP*, FORMER NAVY SEAL JACO Willick wrote about the importance of taking ownership of your mistakes as a leader. Basically, as a leader, you must admit when you screwed up, ask for forgiveness, and try to do better in the future.

When my middle daughter, Lilly, was playing U12 travel softball, there was a team that definitely had our number. We were facing them in the championship of a tournament on their home field. They had defeated us in the previous five games by a combined score of something like 60 to five. It was ugly as we were mercy-ruled (when a team is down by eight runs after five innings, the game ends as a show of mercy) in at least a couple of those games. They were good players and had good coaches, but we knew we were better than the scores of the previous games reflected. This championship was our chance to prove it. We opened the game with an early 2–0 lead in the first inning which was a moral victory for us. In all our past head-to-heads, we never once had a lead. As the game went on, our lead increased, and our defense was doing a tremendous job preventing our opponent from scoring. As we got into the later innings, we had a solid 6–0 lead. We were getting so close to finally breaking the curse this opponent seemed to have put on us.

One thing to note was that this was travel softball, not Little League, which meant there were no rules requiring the coach to play every player in every game. I even explained that distinction to the parents at the beginning of the season. However, I went on to say that in all my years coaching travel softball, I had never had a game in which a girl did not get in the game for at least an inning. What I said was factual, but the parents had never witnessed me using that "no play" option until this game. Despite a

6–0 lead with only a few outs remaining, I kept my starting nine players in the game until the last out. While I did not, technically, do anything wrong or break any rules, I really hurt the girls who didn't play in that big game.

I am not trying to promote the "everyone always gets to play equally" or "everyone gets a trophy" mentality. In fact, I think both are destructive to learning how to compete in the real world. But on that day, in that game, I could have handled things better. Looking back, I realized that those two girls going in for the sixth or seventh inning was extremely unlikely to cost us a six-run lead.

In my long career as a business owner, I have had several occasions that forced me to put my tail between my legs and humbly ask for forgiveness. I am guessing that you have, too. Did you apologize, or did you decide that you are the boss, so whatever happened is "their problem"?

Shortly after I became sales manager at Volk Packaging, I came up with an idea to grow our sales. Since my outside sales representatives were so busy trying to service all of our existing customers, there was little time to prospect and try to grow new business. In our world, it is not uncommon to make 100 cold calls that result in only one actual appointment with a prospect. And it may not even be a very good prospect! I decided that I would hire someone in the role of inside sales. His or her job would be to spend every day pounding the phones (and soon, emails) in an effort to get the outside sales representatives in the door for a meeting.

I found someone right in my factory who seemed like a great fit for this new position. His name was Paul Cote. He was about 24 years old, had a great personality, lots of drive, and was very funny. I hired him, trained him, and put him to work making calls. He was unbelievable! He was making appointment after appointment for the sales team and sometimes even closing new business right on the phone without even involving anyone else. He far exceeded all of my expectations. So, when a position as an on-the-road sales representative became available, I offered the job to him. It seemed like a "slam dunk."

He was so good on the phones I imagined he would be a rock star on the road. Well, the opposite happened. Paul was like a deer in headlights when face to face with customers and prospects. All of the dynamism and success on the phone did not translate when across the desk from someone. It was painful to watch. We tried and tried to work with him, but even he freely admitted that he was terrified to make face-to-face sales calls. I had no choice but to terminate him because we had already filled his inside sales job. Thankfully, I was able to refer Paul to a customer who hired him for phone sales only, and today he is one of the most successful salespeople that I know in any business. But I owed him an apology. I screwed up. I did not take the time and effort to give him a trial run as an outside sales rep. I took the easy route, promoted him, and hired someone else for inside sales. (His replacement never came close to Paul's success and was gone within a year.) I later grabbed lunch with Paul so I could apologize for being lazy and unprofessional in the process of promoting him. I felt like I set him up for failure.

Returning to our championship game, I later met with the parents and players that I knew I had disappointed and apologized for letting my zest for victory derail me from what I knew was the right thing to do. As a coach and as a boss, I've had plenty of opportunities to admit when I've screwed up. And whatever business you're in, you'll get that opportunity, too.

Action Plan

Look back at a time or two when you could have done things better and apologize to whoever you may have hurt.

11

FIND A GOOD MENTOR

I WAS SCARED TO DEATH THE FIRST TIME I COACHED A TRAVEL SOFTBALL GAME. I had coached a local recreation center team for a couple of years while in college, but it was very low key, and most of the girls had no aspirations to play serious softball later in life. However, my first travel softball team, the U10 Southern Maine Flame, was a different story. The girls on the team wanted to learn and get better.

Adding to the pressure was the fact that two of the players on the team had fathers who were already well-established and successful high school coaches, and another had a father who would later go on to coach in high school. Me? I was just the guy who our local high school coach and founder of the travel organization had convinced to coach a travel team by noting that my daughter was "a good little ballplayer." What dad wouldn't want to encourage his child in every way he could? I wound up being the head coach and eventually president of the organization for almost 10 years. Before my first season, however, I was very concerned that I would get to a tournament and make a suggestion only to have one of those experienced coach dads say, "Hey, why are you teaching my kid to play that way?" I needed help, and fast.

Scarborough High School varsity coach Tom Griffin was a great mentor to me, but at that time, he was busy getting his high school team prepared. He didn't have time to babysit me. Meanwhile, I didn't feel comfortable asking too many questions. I was afraid that I would look stupid and make him wonder why he asked me to coach in the first place, which was a fair question. As the well-known saying goes, "Better to remain silent and be thought a fool than to speak and to remove all doubt."

These were the days before YouTube, so I decided to turn to the wonders of VHS. I bought every softball video I could find in the softball product catalogs. I bought videos by softball legends Michelle Smith, Jennie Finch, Dot Richardson, Arizona coach Mike Candrea, and UCLA coach Sue Enquist. I watched them repeatedly, feverishly taking notes in preparation for the next practice because I wanted to be ready for when one of the "softball dads" asked me why I was teaching his daughter a certain way. I figured I would be in the clear if I said, "I learned it that way in a video with Michelle Smith," or "That's how Dot Richardson teaches it." As successful as those guys were at their high schools, I knew they couldn't argue with the legends of the game that I was taking my instruction tips from. Interestingly, in all my years as a softball coach, the situation I feared so much never happened. I guess I was teaching them the right way to play softball.

I can still remember so much from those videos. To this day, I have a really hard time attending a youth softball game and not jumping the fence to show a young player the right way to bunt or how to stand at first base, awaiting the pitch to be released. Once a coach, always a coach. And the same thing happens in the business world. When I see a sales representative with a customer saying the wrong thing, or not saying the right thing, it is also almost impossible for me to stay quiet. And I learned it all from my mentors—video and otherwise.

I have had some amazing mentors in my career. I would never be where I am today had it not been for the guidance of the people at Volk Packaging who taught me the business and how to be a good and effective businessperson. My primary mentor has always been my father. Through watching him, I learned so many of the lessons that enabled me to succeed on the softball field and in the box business, especially about how to care about people. There are plenty of people who act like they care about people and put on a good show, but my father always demonstrated what truly caring about people looks like. Many of the chapters in this book were written due to lessons I garnered from my father. I am forever grateful for that, and I hope I passed some of those lessons along to my children. Even today, over 30 years into my career and well established as a successful businessman, I still reach out to my father (he is 85 as of this writing) whenever I need advice. Dad has been out of the day-to-day workforce for a couple of decades, so he doesn't always give me the best advice for the times we live in, but it is always advice with my best interest at heart. For that reason alone, I will always call him first.

There were three other amazing mentors who influenced my career in different ways. I spent 27 years working side-by-side with my uncle Douglas. He is a very different person than my father and me. He thinks things through more than we do, he likes to get the buy-in of the team, and he contemplates decisions much more methodically than my father or me. That is something I needed to learn. I still make decisions much more quickly than Doug ever did, but he definitely slowed me down in a good way. He taught me to analyze decisions and consider all the outcomes, including unexpected collateral damage. Those were important lessons that have served me well.

Two others who helped form my leadership style were Vice President of Operations Mike Rousselle and Senior Sales Representative Greg Milligan. Mike taught me countless lessons about how to provide the best customer service possible, and Greg groomed me into an effective and productive salesman that I would not be without him. I *may* have figured out a lot of the leadership skills that I have today on my own—or maybe not. I am sure that having my father, Doug, Mike, and Greg—all excellent mentors who wanted to impart their knowledge, wisdom, and experience—got me a lot further than I would have ever made it on my own.

Action Plan

Find someone to be your mentor. Some people think they are too old for a mentor. I would challenge that assertion. I do not believe anyone is too old or too experienced to still learn from others. We can also learn from their failures as much as from their successes. If you insist you are too old for a mentor, find someone to mentor. But optimally, do both.

12

SOMETIMES YOU MUST GET AWAY AND DISCONNECT

BURNOUT IS A COMMON PHRASE USED BY BUSINESS EXECUTIVES. IT ALSO happens with coaches. Being a coach is not an easy job. There is constant pressure to win, to be a good role model, and to remain professional all while sometimes dealing with unreasonable parents, unethical coaches in the other dugout, and bad umpires. The life of a business executive has many of the same pressure pitfalls. You must work with stockholders and/or investors who are always expecting you to win more business so they make more money, as well as unreasonable employees who think you are a money tree and who forget that promotions and bonuses are earned, not given away. There are unethical customers and vendors and a seemingly endless stream of new government regulations. Coaches and business executives may have different reasons for burnout, but I am sure you can see strong similarities.

The battle against burnout for the leader of any organization, from a softball team to a Fortune 500 company to a small enterprise like Volk Packaging, requires careful and premeditated effort. Some people suggest putting your phone in a basket when you walk in the door at home or when you enjoy a nice vacation. The problem is you may need that phone later in the evening to get a text that your teenager is running late. And as great as that vacation is, returning to hundreds of emails and dozens of voicemails can often make you wish you had just stayed home. Another suggestion is to take a few moments in the day with your office door closed to practice mindfulness (yes, I tried that for a while), and while that may work well for some people, the weight of everything going on around you makes relaxing at work extremely challenging and possibly unrealistic.

For my burnout a few years ago, I came up with a pretty good solution. I call it my "vacation phone." It is a basic phone with texting and calling onto which I did not load my email or any social media. Only a couple of people at my office have the number, and they know it is for emergencies only. I used this phone a lot when my kids were still playing competitive sports. When my middle daughter had a softball game, I would often find myself reaching for my primary phone as soon as the inning ended. Before I knew it, I was deep into the email rabbit hole. I frequently looked up from my device only to ask, "Hey, how did we get a girl on second base?" This habit also kept me from getting to know the other parents because, instead of making conversation, I had my face glued to a screen.

When I told my wife about my vacation phone idea, she didn't understand it. She said, "Why don't you just put it on airplane mode during games?" This was a legitimate question. My answer was just as legitimate: "Because I can't. I'm addicted. I am like a crack head with this thing. If I know it is in my pocket and it is a workday (or maybe even if it isn't), I am going to check it. I can't stop myself. I wish I could." I had to figure out how to set boundaries that I could follow. Leaving my primary phone in the car allowed me to truly relax and enjoy the game. I realize not everyone has the financial means to have two phones, but I hope you can find some kind of workaround to take some time, at least somewhat, off the grid. Even if the breaks are short lived, take some time to disconnect.

I always suggest to coaches that they do the same thing with their team. At the end of the season, I encouraged them to take at least a couple of weeks to break away from the sport. I once read that former Florida and Ohio State National Champion college football coach Urban Myer left his team's national championship celebration to sneak into a quiet room in order to make calls to recruits. He lacked an off switch, which eventually wore him down mentally and physically, taking a huge toll on his professional and personal life.

Whatever is happening at the office will almost definitely be there waiting for you when you return. In most cases, whatever it was that seemed so incredibly urgent was something that could have waited. The one thing that I can guarantee you is incredibly urgent is your children growing up much faster than you realize. As the father of four adult children, I can tell you that before you know it, you will be at a high school or college graduation with tears streaming down your cheeks, wondering where the heck all the time went. As the old saying goes, no one ever said on their deathbed, "I wish I spent more time at the office." So, take the time to disconnect. It's worth it.

Action Plan

Get a "vacation phone" or figure out some way you can disconnect every now and then. Find out where you're having trouble disconnecting from work and having trouble setting boundaries. Brainstorm, maybe with your family, some ways you can be intentional about setting boundaries. Trust me, you'll be so happy you did.

13

CATCH COMPETITORS NOT PAYING ATTENTION

WHEN I WAS A KID PLAYING LITTLE LEAGUE, I HAD HORRIBLE COACHING. I had one coach who was a drunk, not far off from Walter Matthau's character in *The Bad News Bears.* And to make matters worse, my team wasn't much better than the Bad News Bears. In three years of Little League, we won five games. To clarify—we did not win five games per year. We won five games in three years! It was pretty pathetic. In fact, our Little League district actually created a mercy rule thanks to my team. When I was 12 years old, in my last year of Little League, we were losing 32 to 2 in only the third inning. There was no mercy rule in the league at the time. The game was eventually called due to darkness, not because we were losing by 30 runs in only three innings. Just a few days later, the district created a mercy rule stating that a team losing by 15 runs was enough to call the game. Sadly, that is my claim to fame from playing Little League—my team was so bad that they created a mercy rule for us.

During my Little League experience, I never had a coach teach me how to effectively win a game. In fact, we never learned any strategy at all. It was only when I became a coach many years later and watched what other coaches were doing to beat my team that I learned an effective strategy to win a game. One of those very small yet effective tactics was running to second base on a walk. For those of you who are not baseball or softball fans, I'll explain. When a player walks after receiving four bad pitches, she generally just goes to first base. Many times, she literally walks to first base. Then one day, I was coaching girls' softball when one of the opposing players got a base on balls, another name for a walk. However, when my catcher very casually tossed the ball back to the pitcher and my pitcher very casually received that ball, never looking over to first base, the runner sprinted straight to second base.

My pitcher had no idea what was going on, my second baseman and shortstop were in their positions between first and second and second and third, and to be honest, I wasn't paying much attention either. But the 10-year-old girl on the other team had been coached very well, so she knew that when you draw a walk, if nobody's paying attention and nobody's covering second base, you can run right to second base. I had no idea what had just happened. When I looked up and saw the girl standing confidently on second base, I turned to my assistant coach and asked, "How did she get to second base?" He looked at me, very confused himself, and simply said, "She ran there." I had not learned the rule that as long as you don't stop at first base, as long as you continue your forward motion, you can proceed to second base. Heck, if the other team is truly not paying attention, a player could run all the way to third base. I learned a very important lesson that day: When the competition is not paying attention, take action!

We do this all the time in business. Sometimes it is done without even thinking about it. If you prepare for the possibility of catching your competition not paying attention, then you are able to take more aggressive action when it happens. My small, privately-owned manufacturing company competes every day against multi-billion-dollar companies. That is not easy to do. These companies have deep pockets, more resources, often better machinery, and, due to their volume, lower prices. But what they often do not have are enough people paying attention. Sometimes these behemoth companies just expect to get the business because they have so much to offer that a small company like mine may not have available. That is when knowing how to see a competitor napping on the job becomes your strategic advantage.

When I was on the road as a sales representative, there was a company in central Maine that I had been calling on for months with no success. When I first called the owner of that company, he told me that I could not come in to see him because he did not like our former salesman. Even though I explained to the owner that some of the reasons he did not like the former salesman were the same reasons he was no longer with Volk Packaging, it was not enough to convince the owner to let me in the door. So, I waited. And I waited some more. And then I waited a little longer. I bided my time, hoping that I could eventually catch my competitor not paying attention and, figuratively, take second base.

Finally, an opportunity presented itself. The prospect called to ask me if I could come in to take a look at their boxes because they were failing. I was so excited to finally get my chance. When I went into the prospect, with the expectation of seeing some inferior boxes that had been delivered to them, I noticed something very different. There was nothing wrong with the boxes. The problem was the manner with which they stacked the boxes. Without getting into a lot of technical details about corrugated boxes that you wouldn't be very interested in reading about, I knew this was my opportunity to pick up a customer I had been working on for a long time. How had the competition not noticed when visiting this customer that they were stacking the boxes incorrectly?

I had to say to the owner of this small camping supply products company that as much as I wanted to claim that my competitor's boxes were of poor quality, I did not think there was anything wrong with the boxes. The problem was that they were not stacking them correctly, causing the boxes to fail. I then gave them a lesson on how to properly stack my competitors' boxes on a pallet, and sure enough, their problem went away. The result of this visit was even better than I expected. Through my honesty and ability to show the customer what my competitor had missed through lack of attention, the customer had enough confidence in me to give me my first order. That was almost 30 years ago, and to this day, we still have all that company's box business. All because I caught my competition not paying attention.

Action Plan

Help your sales team run straight to second base on a walk by getting them together and discussing all the possibilities and scenarios in which you can catch your competition not paying attention.

14

DON'T SWING A BAT THAT'S TOO HEAVY

BEFORE I STARTED COACHING GIRLS SOFTBALL, I HAD NEVER GIVEN MUCH thought to the bats that players used. I had no idea how much weight or how big a bat should be used for a 9-, 10-, 11-, or 12-year-old girl. In time, I learned what bat was appropriate for the different age levels in size and strength for a youth softball player.

I'll never forget when a 10-year-old girl on my Little League team showed up to a game with the brand-new $300 bat that her parents had recently bought her. She was so excited to show me her new bat and get into the batter's box with it. I picked up the bat and read the length and weight of it. It was a 34-inch bat. That was what they call a drop 10. In softball terms, "drop" indicates how much less the bat weighs, numerically, as compared to the length. Her bat was 34 inches long and 24 ounces. That size bat was significantly too long and too heavy for any 10-year-old girl. In fact, it was too heavy for most high school players.

I felt awful when I had to inform her that her bat was beautiful, but she would need to put it away and not swing it until she was probably a sophomore or junior in high school, and maybe not even then. She looked at me with such disappointment, but there was little chance that she would ever get a hit with a bat so big and so heavy at age 10. I felt even more awkward when I had to escort her over to the bleachers and hand the bat to her parents, explaining why I would not allow her to use her new gift. Unfortunately, they had already ripped the protective plastic off the top of the bat, so they would not even be able to return it for an appropriately-sized bat. I said to the parents, "I hate to tell you this, and I hate to tell her even more, but I can't let her use this bat because she'll never be able to get it around fast enough to do anything with it." I told her parents it was a generous gift, but she would unfortunately need to wait many years to use it. The parents were disappointed, but they understood my position with the bat and appreciated that I did not allow their daughter to fail at the plate because her bat was way too heavy.

It is very important to understand what your company's capabilities are. If you don't know what your business can do well and what it cannot do at all, it is very possible that you, or someone on your team, will try to swing a bat that is way too heavy. The consequences of overpromising and underdelivering could cost your company time, money, and reputation.

What might a bat that's too big for you be in the business world? Well, in my company we jokingly refer to the phrase, "That's right up our alley!" This comment has gained legendary status at Volk Packaging. This phrase became a sort of cliche about 20 years ago when my uncle, who was my business partner at the time, visited a customer who had a product which was extremely heavy. The box that the customer wanted to buy was a triple wall box with a double wall liner glued on the inside of it. A corrugated box is a box with the squiggly paper in between each layer. (The next time you go to a supermarket in the summer and see those large boxes that sit on pallets and are full of watermelons, check it out. Those boxes are probably what I'm describing in this story.) The box this customer wanted had five rows of the squiggly paper. My company sold triple wall boxes, and we sold double wall boxes. What we could not do was manufacture a triple wall box with a double wall box glued on the inside of it.

The customer asked my sales representative and my uncle if we could quote that exact box. Before my uncle was able to speak up, my salesperson looked the customer straight in the eye and said, "That's right up our alley!" No one knows to this day what alley he was working in because we did not have the machinery to make such a box. He had put my uncle in an awkward position, as he had to correct the optimistic sales representative in front of the customer so as to not walk away with a customer expecting us to quote something that we could not produce. He is an amazing salesperson, but that day, he was swinging a bat that was too heavy for him.

Action Plan

If you are the leader of an organization, you or someone you delegate might want to create a training program for your team that educates them on what you do well and what is not up your alley. Your team must understand what you can do successfully and what you cannot do. As a leader within an organization, part of your job is to ensure that none of your players are trying to swing a bat that is too heavy.

15

LOOK FOR DIAMONDS IN THE ROUGH

ANYONE WHO HAS COACHED A TEAM IN ANY SPORT LEARNS VERY QUICKLY which players are potential stars and which players will take some work. It usually takes less than a single practice to discover this information, but sometimes it takes time to sweep away the dirt and find the diamonds.

When I was coaching a U12 travel softball team in 2007, we picked up a new player named Julia Geaumont. Julia was from the neighboring town and had not played travel softball before, so we had no idea who she was when she arrived at tryouts. Even her dad said to me, "Julia thinks she is a pitcher, but she just started pitching lessons, so please don't feel obligated to pitch her in real games." It is very unusual for a dad to say something like that. Most dads say something more like, "Hey, Coach, I just wanted you to know that my kid is quite possibly the greatest player that has ever stepped on a field and could, in fact, be superhuman." I would like to say that this example is a gross exaggeration, but anyone who has coached youth sports knows it is not that far from accurate.

My assistant coaches and I heeded the dad's advice for a little while, until we got to know Julia and saw her talent. She had tremendous potential and, on top of her raw talent, was one of the hardest working girls I had ever seen. She was determined to move up the pitching rotation and worked tirelessly at practices and at home to improve her skills. By the time we reached the U14 level, Julia was pitching some of the biggest games of the season. She later went on to win both Miss Softball Maine and Maine Gatorade Player of the Year while in high school before going on to pitch at Bowdoin College. What would have happened with Julia's career if we had accepted that she was a marginal player and would never rise above that?

Similar situations happen in the business world all the time. Leaders are presented with scenarios that allow them to either include their whole team or just focus on the high performers. Our instinct, and the advice of many business leadership experts, is to focus on the most successful team members. I have read those books and articles, and I understand the thought process. However, by never giving the time and attention to the people who appear to be mid-level performers, you never have the opportunity to see if they can thrive when the pressure is on. Remember that guy named Tom Brady? He started his career as the 199th pick of the draft but went on to become one of the greatest quarterbacks, if not *the* greatest quarterback, ever.

At Volk Packaging, we take great pride in stories of people rising through the ranks to positions of higher authority, more responsibility, and better incomes. Often your greatest potential employees are right under your nose. However, they must be given the opportunity to make the most of the moment when their time arrives. Many companies are more comfortable bringing in someone from the outside with pre-established credentials and experience, thereby missing the hidden gems within their own ranks. While it is true that it is generally safer to find a proven entity, what those companies and leaders who go that route will never experience is the thrill of seeing someone reach unexpected heights, excelling beyond what they even thought possible themselves. If you have been ignoring someone in your company, take another look at them. You may have had a diamond in your midst who has never been given a chance to shine.

Action Plan

Does your company perform performance reviews? Have you created job descriptions for every role in the company? If not, start by doing these two tasks. They could be a great way to find a diamond in the rough. Additionally, take some chances on some people. Give people opportunities, assuming they want the additional responsibility, to fail. The most important part of this Action Plan is accepting that sometimes it does not work out as you hoped. I suggest allowing them a long enough leash to stretch themselves but being there to support them so they do not hang themselves. You might just discover the next unexpected hero in your company.

16

BUILD A STRONG FARM TEAM

THE 1996 NEW YORK YANKEES WON 125 GAMES WITHOUT A SINGLE PLAYER making the All-Star team or hitting 30 home runs. They didn't buy their way to all those victories, as many teams do today, by trading for or acquiring the most expensive players through free agency. They accomplished this amazing feat by building an incredible farm team program. A farm team program consists of all the teams that are within the organization but are not the "big leagues." For example, in Portland, Maine, we have the Portland Sea Dogs. They are a farm team for the Boston Red Sox. A good Little League system is considered a farm team for high school programs. The legendary New York Yankees won several World Series in the late 1990s with previously unknown players like Derek Jeter, Mariano Rivera, Jorge Posada, and Paul O'Neill.

Tom Griffin, the Maine high school softball coach that I mentioned earlier in the book, was a genius when it came to building a farm program. He ran after-school clinics for young players starting at age five or six. He started a Sunday pitching clinic to coax girls into being pitchers early in their softball life. Every March (just before Little League started), Coach Griffin hosted a four-part series of lessons with instruction on topics from hitting and catching to sliding and bunting. He even started a summer camp for girls to come learn about softball and invited high school players (celebrities to the young Little Leaguers) to help with the drills and instruction. What do you think happened when those little girls found out their new high school buddy from camp was playing a game? Of course, they wanted to go watch the game. This brought even more enthusiasm for the game of softball to these budding state champ hopefuls. (See Chapter 11 on mentorship). Finally, Coach Griffin identified passionate parents like me to join the sport and then proceeded to teach us his way of coaching softball so the girls had consistency from age eight to 18.

When I was hired to coach the Scarborough (Maine) Middle School team, Coach Griffin handed me his coaching "bible" with strict instructions to not show it or share it with anyone! This was a responsibility that I took very seriously. No player saw the book, and I only occasionally shared parts of it with my assistant coach. It was all the things he taught the high school girls. He was adamant, and I never questioned him, that I teach them exactly what they would learn when they reached high school. Every sign, every strategy, every movement of every player in virtually every game scenario was carefully written down for me to instruct the middle schoolers. No player coming up the ranks in that district would ever get to Coach Griffin's high school practice and say, "That's not what Coach Volk told me in middle school." That consistency played a major role in his success in winning eight state championships in Class A Maine high school softball.

We have been working with that same model at Volk Packaging for several years. As I watched my father and uncle retire, as well as some of my best and most loyal employees, I knew we needed to create a better farm program. We needed a stronger "bench" so that when people left the company or retired, the customer would not notice, and my business would remain stable. The first thing I did was sit down individually with everyone that was at or nearing retirement age. (Of course, as times change and people live longer, the words "retirement age" means something very different to everyone.)

I did not want anyone to feel pressure to retire or have any sense of age discrimination, so every conversation began with, "Let me be very clear. I am not asking you this question because of your performance or anything you did or did not do. I am just working on succession planning, and that task is impossible if I have no idea what everyone is planning regarding retirement. So, do you have a date in mind?" This led to answers ranging from "I am thinking maybe next year" to "I have no plans to retire" to "Beats me."

I also started hiring what we termed "junior sales representatives" to help with the succession of my sales team. These salespeople were given a territory of small customers. By only working with smaller clients, they have been able to increase their knowledge and skills with very little pressure or fear of making a mistake that could cost us a major account. This was comforting for them and for me! Slowly, over time, we have started transitioning larger and more significant customers to them. In addition, the junior sales representatives have covered for the older reps when they take time off, allowing the customers to get to know the younger members of the team in a more casual way. As the more experienced salespeople have been ready to retire, the customers have more smoothly transitioned to the junior salespeople. While there are still further steps needed in succession planning, the salesperson succession plan was the first step in ensuring that Volk Packaging has a capable farm team to make major personnel changes essentially seamless to the customers.

Action Plan

Go through your employee roster and begin a plan for succession of key people. Those key people do not have to be seniors or near seniors. It could be a 43-year-old who has skills that would be very difficult to replace. You also want to seek out individuals within your organization who you or other leaders see as having good potential to move up the ladder. Those rising stars and diamonds in the rough should be growing through your farm team. Discover where your organization is vulnerable, and then start building your farm system.

17

LISTEN WITH CAUTION TO THOSE OUTSIDE THE GAME

BEST-SELLING AUTHOR AND EXECUTIVE COACH, JOHN BRUBAKER, OFTEN TALKS about how some of the best ideas come from people outside the business. I don't disagree with that, but you must make sure that person has at least a basic concept and understanding of some of the complexities of your business.

When I was a softball coach, hardly a game or practice or conversation with a parent did not involve some kind of advice about how I could be a better coach. With parents especially, the advice usually revolved around how I could better coach their child. Many times, the advice was helpful because they knew their children better than I did. Parents often know the best way in which to explain something or motivate their child, my player. However, when parents who rarely even attended games and never stayed to observe practices attempted to offer advice, I took it with a grain of salt. Even then, I rarely got offended when parents would make suggestions. I always tried to give them the benefit of the doubt that they were trying to be helpful to the team and to me. Of course, I knew sometimes that was true and sometimes it was not true.

As a coach, you must process parent information, as well as friendly advice, and decide whether it will benefit the player and/or the team. Unfortunately, in some cases, the advice would come from someone who did not understand the game. Often, subtle nuances make the difference between winning or losing. Usually, the advice parents had for me about how to motivate or teach their child was informative, but the instruction on how to manage the game was not so helpful.

While I don't know you, what I do know is that there are some inherent theories of leading a team that I have learned over the years which are universal in the business world and on the softball field. Whether you are just starting a business or have been running your company successfully for 30 years as I have, people who don't have a clue about your business are sure to give you advice. Listen to what they say. You never know who might have a terrific idea. But listen with caution. At the end of the day, make sure your decisions are filtered by your understanding of your company, customers, employees, and competition. Your golf buddy or neighbor may have some interesting perspectives, but it is likely that he does not have an in-depth understanding of those critical aspects. So, it does not matter if you are running a large business or a small business or starting up a small at-home company—be careful who you take advice from.

Action Plan

Seek advice from people outside your company with wisdom and experience, but be careful about listening to people who have opinions on everything, even things they know nothing about.

18

PICK THE PLAYERS WITH THE RIGHT ATTITUDE, NOT JUST THE RIGHT SKILLS

EVERYONE KNEW CASSANDRA WAS A GOOD FIELDER. EVERYONE KNEW Cassandra had a rocket for an arm. When tryouts came after the end of my daughter's U10 season, it was assumed that Cassandra would be on the U12 team. However, my coaches and I saw something in Cassandra that the fans, other parents, and especially her mother did not see. Cassandra's attitude … well, it sucked.

My assistant coach for many years while I was coaching, a wonderful guy named Tim Hannan, and I were coaching the 10 and under (U10) Southern Maine Flame and moving up with our daughters to the 12 and under (U12) level. Advancing from U10 to U12 is probably the biggest jump in skills of any age adjustment for the girls. Pretty much any girl can play U10, but at U12, they have to have some skills.

At that time, Manny Ramirez was the left fielder for the Boston Red Sox, and both Tim and I were big Red Sox fans. Manny was famous for sometimes giving half the effort. If there was a ground ball to shortstop and he knew he was probably going to get out, he would barely leave the batter's box or just casually jog to first base holding his bat. At one point, a reporter asked him about it, and his response was, "I'm just Manny being Manny." We used to call Cassandra "Little Manny." (Never to her face or anyone else, of course—just between us as she was only 11 years old.) If she hit a ground ball that she thought was an easy out, she wouldn't run. If she had a pop fly that she thought would be caught—and let me be very clear that there's no such thing as an easy out at the U10 level—she wouldn't run. And worst of all, if Cassandra was put in a position that she did not want to play or a position that she felt was beneath her skill level, she gave a half-hearted effort at best.

So, when tryouts came for the U12 team, we had a big decision to make. Should we pick the 12 best players at the tryouts, knowing one of those players would be Cassandra? Or should we choose the 11 best players and replace Cassandra with a girl who had less skill but a better attitude? Tim and I didn't need a lot of discussion before we agreed that Cassandra would not be on the U12 team. It was a difficult decision because I had to decide whether or not to explain to Cassandra, or her mom, why she was not chosen.

This conversation was unlikely to go well because her mother did not see what we saw and knew that Cassandra was going to be one of the 12 best players at the tryouts. For days, I weighed the decision of what to tell or not tell them. Note that I didn't waiver on the decision whether to pick Cassandra. I struggled with how to best communicate the reasons for the decision to her and her mom. After the tryouts, I decided honesty was the best policy. I could not think of a way to explain to her mom why we did not choose Cassandra without addressing her attitude because it was obvious to everyone that she clearly had the skills to play on the U12 team.

I knew very well that when I talked to her mother and described how Cassandra's negative attitude and lack of effort had caused her to be cut from the team, she would be very angry with me, and she was. However, I was also hoping that perhaps someday when the second, third, or fourth coach said the same thing about Cassandra, maybe her mom would look back and think to herself, *I guess that Derek wasn't such a jerk after all.* I knew that I would never know if that happened because there was no chance I would get a phone call from her mom telling me that I made the right decision back when Cassandra was 11. It has been 18 years, and that call has not come. I am still confident that Tim and I made the right decision for the team and possibly even for Cassandra's growth as a young person.

When hiring, firing, and promoting people in your business, think about Cassandra. Hire, fire, and promote based on attitude as much as skill and performance. Of course, skills and performance matter, but I will take a marginal performer with average skills and a great attitude over a workplace "Cassandra" every day of the week.

Back in the early 2000s we had a customer service representative who was a workplace "Cassandra." I'll call her Andrea. Andrea was a good worker and had an amazing relationship with our biggest customer. However, her attitude was awful. In her view, everything was about Andrea. She was the best, and everyone else should take a backseat to whatever she wanted. We put up with her antics for as long as we felt we could manage it, but eventually, her behavior was impacting the work experience for the entire department. People literally did not want to come to work because of Andrea. She had to go. We terminated her employment and, to our surprise, kept the big customer. We had overvalued her role with them. They loved Volk Packaging and had no intention of changing box suppliers, even after Andrea's sudden departure. Everyone in the department, and many others across the company, were thankful when she left. And I never regretted it.

Action Plan

When you are choosing employees to join your company, for promotions, or even to take on important projects, remember that attitude always matters. We try to hire people based on our core values: customer-centricity, accountability, respect, and excellence. If potential employees have those core values, we know that success within the organization is much more likely.

19

REAL LIFE DOESN'T GIVE OUT PARTICIPATION TROPHIES

THE BANE OF MY YEARS COACHING LITTLE LEAGUE WERE THE PARTICIPATION trophies they made me hand out. I had to give a trophy to kids who missed games, kids who didn't even try, and kids who had crappy attitudes. I had to give trophies to players on a team that barely won any games. I know this will upset some people, but I think that's ridiculous. Participation trophies not only reward kids for underachieving and taint the value of an actual earned trophy, but they also teach kids that you get a prize just for showing up. Do you know what you get in business for showing up? Nothing!

This topic has been discussed at length in other books and articles (and I'm sure on social media), so I will not dwell on it in this book, but I did not feel I could write a book about softball and business without addressing the hard fact that you get squat for just showing up. Heck, in Little League, the kids got a trophy even if they only showed up half the time. I used to wonder why we didn't save the coaches the effort at the end of the season and just give the kids a trophy in February when they registered for the upcoming season. But that is not how the real world works. The reality of life is, or should be, merit based.

A giant myth today is that you should get what you think you deserve. You do not get what you think you deserve in sports (beyond Little League) or business. You get what you actually earn through accomplishing something! So, stop expecting a reward for showing up and do not allow that culture in your company. Effort matters. Getting along with others matters. Completing tasks on time and correctly does matter. Performance matters.

Action Plan

Make sure your company has a merit-based rewards and promotion system. If someone thinks they will get a prize for just showing up to work, quickly explain to them how the real world works. Share with them, in detail, if possible, what they have to accomplish to reach their goals. And then help them be the best they can be.

20

MIX UP SPEEDS

ONE OF THE MOST IMPORTANT SKILLS THAT A SOFTBALL PITCHER MUST HAVE is the ability to vary pitching speeds. If the pitcher throws with the same speed every time, by the third or fourth inning, the other team will have an expectation of how fast the pitch will be coming to them. Once the batter can time the pitch, it becomes much easier for them to start making contact. The ability to throw multiple pitches, such as curveballs and screw balls, is also critical to a softball pitcher's success. A pitcher acquires a significant advantage if she has the skill to throw a 60-mile-per-hour fastball followed by a 47-mile-per-hour change-up. The goal in varying pitches and speeds is to create mental chaos for the batter.

When my daughter got to college, her pitching coach would call the same exact pitch to batter after batter, inning after inning. As expected, the other team figured out quickly what was coming at them. It was then just a matter of making an adjustment to the timing and movement of the ball, since they knew both, and swinging their bat according to that intel.

The same concept is vital for a successful business, especially entrepreneurs, start-ups, or businesses that have a lot of competition. I have always told my sales representatives that if every customer we visit hears the same sales pitch from us, it is only a matter of time before that sales pitch is familiar to our competitors. If my salesperson repeats the same thing to prospect after prospect, it will not be long before a prospective customer, or two or three, most of whom already have a cozy relationship with their current suppliers, relays that pitch to our competitors. If your competition realizes that your company has just one sales pitch, they can easily plan how to beat you. Every prospect must be looked at and sold to based on their personal needs, expectations, and requirements. There is generally no one-size-fits-all for your prospects and customers.

In our business, we must "mix up speeds." We may talk to one customer about warehousing and vendor management of their inventory. At the next prospect, we may be presenting a solution based on just-in-time deliveries. And for another, packaging design could be the big challenge to address. Telling every potential customer the same exact thing, or even a slight variation of the same thing, is like throwing a fastball on every pitch. Before long, you will start giving up hits, and probably hard ones. The likelihood of giving up hits, on the softball field or to business competitors, often comes down to how well you can mess with the timing of the person trying to hit off you.

Action Plan

Look at your customer base and make a list of how you can customize your services based on their needs instead of your wants.

21

KNOW YOUR COMPETITIONS' STRENGTHS AND WEAKNESSES

KNOWING YOUR COMPETITIONS' STRENGTHS AND WEAKNESSES IS PROBABLY the most obvious crossover between work and softball. The famous Chinese general Sun Tzu said, "Know thy enemy." When I was a softball coach, every chance we had to see the next team we would be playing, my coaches and I took. We made notes as we tracked who the big hitters were, what player liked to chase the high pitches, which girls could anticipate a changeup, and who was afraid of a rising inside screwball. We wanted to know which players were threats on the base paths and which ones never seemed to make an error. And then we tried to exploit their weaknesses and work around their strengths.

It is important to study your competition in business as well. At Volk Packaging, we want to know who has great customer service, who has no flexibility with their customer's demands, and what machines our competitors have—even more importantly, what can they do that we cannot. As one of my salespeople likes to say, "Do your homework, and you'll do well on the test."

Once a year we update a document that we call "Know the Competition." My sales representatives and I go through every other company in our market that sells boxes in an effort to determine their strengths and weaknesses. The one rule we have when updating the document is that no one is allowed to say pricing because the fact is on any given day, any one of the dozens of companies selling boxes in our market could present lower prices to our customers in an effort to steal our business. Every salesperson could throw out an anecdote about a time when this competitor or that competitor offered our customer a lower price and "stole" a customer from us. If we allowed pricing to be on the sheet, it would probably be listed as a strength for every single competitor. We have the awareness that we could lose business due to pricing at any time, so we must remain competitive in the market.

That being said, the goal of the "Know the Competition" document is for everyone to understand how to best compete when facing each rival, regardless of the pricing. We would never want to go to a potential customer bragging about our printing capability if we are competing against someone with better graphics ability than we have at our company. If we know our potential customer's current supplier has limited space or simply refuses to stock boxes for their customers, we will be sure to mention that we have a stocking program in order to maximize our competitive advantage. Does the competitor have a division or the ability to do 3PL (third party logistics), fulfillment, kitting, and ecommerce? If not, we try to find an avenue for our Volk Paxit division, which is the contract packaging division of Volk Packaging where we offer all of those services and more. We have found that once the customer is utilizing the amazing array of Volk Packaging's box-making capabilities with the incredibly flexible and efficient services of Volk Paxit, our competition shrinks from dozens of companies to very few.

Watch almost any of today's sports on television. How many times do you see a batter strike out or a quarterback throw an interception only to have the camera pan to the player who just made the mistake? What is that player often doing? He or she is looking at an iPad with the at-bat or throw that was just the subject of their very public failure. Why are they watching the painful footage again? To learn! They want to see what the competition did that caused them to fail in that moment. Was the batter looking for a fastball but receiving an off-speed curveball? Did the quarterback completely miss that the safety was watching the quarterback's eyes the entire play, anticipating where the pass would go? How did those professional athletes miss such critical information? They lacked the proper intel about the other team. They were missing important pieces of knowledge that can make or break a game—knowledge that can turn a win into a loss.

Knowledge is power. When attempting to survive in an extremely competitive business (or sports) environment, knowledge is not just power—it is a matter of life or death for your team or your company. Whatever business you are in, I guarantee you will be stronger if you educate yourself and your team about who is targeting your existing customers and selling to the potential customers you want.

Action Plan

Gather your team together to discuss and document all your competitors by creating a list of their strengths and weaknesses.

22

EQUAL AND FAIR ARE NOT THE SAME THING

CAN'T TELL YOU HOW MANY TIMES, IN BUSINESS AND ON THE SOFTBALL FIELD, I've heard someone say, "That isn't fair." When I was a kid and made that statement, my father would say, "Life isn't fair. Not everyone gets treated like Ted Williams."

As a softball coach, I learned that all players are not the same. Some players came and went as they bounced from team to team each season, while other players were with me from age nine to age 18 or older. I coached some girls during the summer while they were in elementary school and later was still coaching them during college summer breaks, whereas some girls I saw for one summer and never saw them again. So, do I give all the same exact rules to the girl who was on my team from nine to 19 as the girl who just showed up that summer? Heck no.

After my second or third year as a travel coach, usually while at a Little League game, I would hear the same kind of comment about tryouts for my travel team. It went something like this: "Don't bother trying out for Derek Volk's team. He's already picked his players." If I had picked my entire team by May when I heard this comment, a full four months prior to the actual tryouts, why would I bother wasting my time holding the tryout? I was always looking for new talent. However, by May it would be fair to say that there were some players I knew would be on my team (assuming they chose to try out for my team again). There were amazing young softball players who I had on my U10 team and maybe U12 team as well. I knew they were awesome because I had been watching them for two or three years. So, did I already know that if those girls appeared at tryouts, I would pick them? Absolutely! In fact, with a couple of them, I went so far as to say, "Don't come to tryouts. I know that I want you on the team, so if you want to play for me again, just say so. I don't need to waste valuable and limited tryout time watching you hit 10 balls or catch pop flies. Your past performance can be the tryout." Then there were other players who I had never seen outside a Little League game or two, or maybe never at all. They had to come to the tryout still in order to be considered for the team. Was that equal treatment? No, but I feel it was fair. It was actually more than fair because it allowed me to give the new girls much more time for a full and thorough tryout instead of rushing them through the process.

The same has been true at Volk Packaging, and probably in your business or organization. Does the employee who has been with us for 25, 30, or even 40 years have to follow all the same rules as the employee who started three months ago? No way. Does that mean I am being unfair to the new employee? It does not.

Of course, some rules are rules that must always be respected. For example, showing up to work on time is critical for all employees. It is not possible to run a large box machine when employees cannot be counted on to arrive on time for their shifts. Our machine operators work extremely hard all day long to keep the machines making boxes, an impossible task if the forklift driver who needs to bring material to and from the machine is an hour late every day. We have a forklift driver who, as of May 16, 2022, set the record for the longest employment ever at our company. At that time, we had been in business for 55 years. Mike Allen had been with us for over 43 of those years! That's an amazing accomplishment. But that does not mean Mike can show up and leave whenever he wants. We do have some rules that everyone must follow. However, if Mike is having a personal situation at home, we are more likely to cut him some slack. Why? Because he earned it. Much like the softball player who had played previous seasons for me, I know what I have with Mike. I know he is hard-working. I know he is dependable. I know that I can count on him when I need him. It is really a very simple concept, and yet, it feels so foreign to many people. Respect is earned, and Mike Allen, after 43 years of dedicated service, has earned my respect. He earned the right to take an extra day off if he needs it. That is why treating everyone fairly is definitely not always equal.

Action Plan

Very few companies, including my own, would ever have a written policy that explains this concept. Because of that, I do not have a hard Action Plan for this chapter. My advice is to just think about how you treat your team to make sure that your rules are fair. Once you feel your company rules are fair, use your instinct, compassion, and your knowledge of each player to decide if "equal" is required. This is a gut decision, not so much a policy idea.

23

DECIDE WHERE YOU
WANT THE TEAM TO GO

EVERY LEADER MUST HAVE A VISION. WHEN YOU'RE A COACH, YOUR TEAM LOOKS to you to give them a vision. They want to know the destination they are striving to reach. What is the big picture? To accomplish that vision, the team and the players need goals. Goals are attainable and measurable targets to go after that lead the team to the greater vision. They want to know what they should accomplish to consider the season or business year a success.

On the softball field, the vision for a team of nine- and 10-year-olds (U10) is going to be very different from the vision at U16 or U18. At U10, the primary objective is to build skills, learn the game, and have fun. It is certainly more fun if you can win some games, or maybe a tournament or two along the way, but the ultimate goal at that age is instilling a love for the game. I used to tell U10 parents that my biggest goal for their daughters was for them to show up at tryouts in September. If I could keep a lacrosse stick out of their hands, I did well.

When I coached older teams, the goal was more about wins and losses, and for some, the goal was getting "seen" by college coaches. Even with the older kids, however, having fun should still be a major part of the vision. I would frequently remind the more competitive, win-at-all-costs parents that 20 years from now, almost none of the girls will have any idea how many games we won or lost. What they will all remember are the relationships they had, the fun experiences they enjoyed with their teammates, and the special bonding time they had with their parents. Coaching youth sports is ultimately the same as coaching employees—it is the relationships that matter most. Relationships need to be part of your business's vision, team, and personal goals.

People work for pay. However, I guarantee you will lose employees much faster if they don't like their coworkers, supervisors, or you! They will also leave your company if they have no idea what the point is. Where is the company going? What is the vision?

To be honest, I have not always done a great job expressing my vision at work. It is a lot easier with a youth softball team. I have found that it takes conscious thought and effort to formulate a vision. It is not something that can be slapped together casually. Your vision will be valued by your employees in direct correlation to the effort you put into it. Additionally, the vision cannot be too easy to achieve because then it will not feel like it has much value, but it cannot be pie in the sky either. It must be challenging but attainable.

I remember the first time I sat down to write my vision for Volk Packaging. I had no idea how to do it, so I bought a book. The book was useless because all it did was talk about companies like Toyota, Google, and Apple. They had examples like, "We want to be the best car company in the world." Another one was, "We want to be the #1 search engine on the planet." I run a small family-owned box company in Biddeford, Maine. Those lofty goals are cool, but I found them completely impossible to relate to. I needed to create a vision that my team could actually see to fruition. How can your team strive for a vision they don't know exists? What is your vision for your team, your department, your company, and for yourself? The vision should be clear but flexible. Our company vision in 1974 was certainly not the same as it is in 2024. Here is the Volk Packaging vision and mission as of January 1, 2024:

Volk Packaging Vision

Volk Packaging will make a positive and lasting impact on the lives of people by creating an exceptional place to work, being a great corporate citizen, thriving financially, and running a company that customers love doing business with.

Volk Packaging Mission Statement

Led by God, managed by a family that cares for our customers, coworkers, and community. Making boxes while making a difference.

Action Plan

Take some time away from the office to craft your business's vision with the reality of your world. Look at where your company is and where you believe it could go. I would suggest involving your leadership team or trusted advisors. And then share it. There are dozens of books that guide you through the process. If you are stumped on how to begin, my recommendation would be to start by reading *Traction* by Gino Wickman.

24

LET YOUR PLAYERS CARRY THEIR OWN BAG

WHEN I WAS A SOFTBALL COACH, ALMOST NOTHING DROVE ME AS CRAZY AS seeing a parent carrying one of my player's bags. Travel softball players are given big bags that hold all their equipment. They can put their gloves, bat, batting gloves, visor, etc. in the bag. When they enter the dugout, they hang the bag, which has built in clips, along the front or back of the dugout. I always told my players, even at U10, that I expected them to carry their own bag from their car to the dugout, and back to their car. Their parents worked hard all week to pay for them to play travel softball and then gave up several summer weekends, when they could have been at the beach or lake, to watch their daughters play. The least the girls could do was carry their own bag because by doing so, they demonstrated responsibility for their own equipment. Parents who carried their kid's bag encouraged them to be both lazy and entitled.

I expect the same from my employees. Discovering that a supervisor or manager did the paperwork for someone who is their subordinate drives me nuts. Sometimes employees do paperwork for coworkers who are peers. I get it. They do so because they want to be helpful. However, the problem with doing someone else's work is the same as parents carrying a player's bag: It creates an employee who is lazy and entitled. Even as the CEO of the company, I occasionally had sales representatives ask me to complete paperwork for them. Could I do it? Sure, I could have done it, and maybe saved the employee some time, but what kind of message would that send? It communicates that my time doing my job is less valued than spending it doing their job. Furthermore, it creates a culture of dependence. Help your employees grow in responsibility and ownership by making sure they are carrying their own bag.

Action Plan

Ask your managers and supervisors if they are doing anything for their subordinates that the subordinates could be doing themselves. Help them learn the critical but challenging art of delegating. As with vision setting, there are countless books about delegating, so I won't try to reinvent the wheel. If you need help getting started with delegating, try reading *Trust and Inspire* by Stephen Covey.

25

COMMUNICATE WHEN PLAYERS THINK THEY ARE BETTER THAN THEY ARE

HAVE OFTEN FOUND THE SIMILARITIES BETWEEN COACHING SOFTBALL PLAYERS and managing employees to be remarkable. Sometimes, if I close my eyes, I might not know if I am talking to a softball player or an employee. I am not saying that in a derogatory manner nor am I meaning to imply that my employees are immature or not adults. What I mean is that I have noticed human nature is human nature. While we all mature as we become adults, there are parts of our brains that shockingly remain the same. I am no scientist or brain expert, but it seems to me that whatever part of the brain dictates confidence in oneself does not change much as we get older.

A softball team will have 12 or 13 players. Even though they are at the same practice as you are, they will most likely interpret their performances very differently from you. In my experience, most of those players will feel they have the skills and the mentality to play whatever position and hit anywhere in the batting order they find most appealing. Even players who may have great insecurities about themselves will truly believe that they should be getting more playing time, playing a different position, or be placed higher in the batting order than the coach may feel is appropriate. The best way to address this dichotomy of opinions is to get an understanding of what the player feels are her strengths, see if she has a realistic view of her weaknesses, and then try to help her assess whether she views herself accurately. To this end, I used to do mid-season reviews with players so I could make sure we were on the same page.

The same is true for your employees. Similar to the inaccurate perceptions that an athlete might have about themselves, an employee may feel like he or she is the hardest-working person in their department, has the capabilities to handle machinery they are not ready to operate, or believe they can solve a customer's problem without any assistance from their coworkers. And just like when you are coaching youth softball, you have to be very thoughtful and sensitive when having these conversations. People do not like to be told that their opinions of themselves are off base. It is simply human nature to not always see ourselves as we truly are. Trust me—I realize that I am throwing stones from a glass house. I am no different. Employees are no different than the youth girls. It's just the way we are wired.

Communication is the key to so many aspects of running a team or a business. Talk to people. Talk to them in person. Don't just rely on texts, emails, or company surveys. The most important thing you can do when it comes to addressing the imbalance between what employees or players think they are capable of and what you or your managers feel they are capable of comes down to open and honest communication. Be truthful about what you see as their weaknesses and skills gaps and ask them a lot of questions about how they see their performance at the company. These can be difficult conversations, but do it anyway.

Keep in mind that it is impossible to avoid conflict between you and your employees 100% of the time when there are differences of opinion about your employees' capabilities. Enter into these conversations knowing that even if you to listen to what they have to say and express openly and honestly how the company staff feels about their capabilities, you may still walk away with different opinions, no matter what you say or how long you talk. Have the conversation anyway! You will be a lot better off.

Action Plan

Instead of conducting regular performance reviews to tell your employees how their job performances are weak or strong, conduct them to determine how much your opinions of their skills and performances match their opinions. A big gap that is not communicated can cost you an employee.

26

SIT NEAR THE DOOR DURING TRYOUTS

WHEN I WAS A NEW LITTLE LEAGUE COACH AT MY FIRST TRYOUTS, I DISCOVERED a great way to choose the right players for my team. I sat near the door to the gym. This little trick came to me by accident, a valuable discovery I made while sitting in the gym, watching all the kids try out for Little League. I was doing what all the other coaches were doing. My checklist in hand, I was scoring kids on a scale from 1 to 5 on their skills in hitting (hits consistently but gets mostly singles), hitting for power (hits more doubles, triples, and home runs), fielding, throwing, and base running. I was looking, as all the other coaches were, for the five-tool player. And then something interesting happened: A kid who had a lot of skills, whom I had given mostly 4s and 5s to on the checklist, exited the gym and slammed her glove on the floor while simultaneously yelling at her parents. She was throwing a true temper tantrum. I have a son with special needs, so I know some kids have meltdowns, but this player had had a pretty good tryout. I could not understand what she was so ticked off about.

After that, I kept watching what happened just outside the door of the gym. I saw a dad yell at his daughter as she left the gym, and another give his daughter a big hug. I saw a dad high-five a girl who had a rather weak tryout and another girl jump for joy. I started looking for both players and parents with good attitudes. Coaching Little League is a voluntary position. I was not getting paid for it, and at the end of the day, no one would remember (except probably me) how many games we won, so why would I want to deal with a bunch of prima donna kids and obnoxious, overbearing parents?

Work is different. It is a paid position. However, no one wants to hire people who will become problems in the office or in the plant. You will not always know what you need to know about a person from a job interview. Like the girls at Little League tryouts, they are making their best effort to show you that they are that five-tool player for your workplace, so you need to find out what's happening when they walk out the door. There are multiple ways you can do that. Always do reference checks, preferably not with the people they list, as those people were set up to say good things. Dig into the resume to find people to call who were not mentioned as references. Scour their social media accounts. Their Facebook, Instagram, and LinkedIn pages will tell you more about the candidate than the interview ever could. As they say, "Hire slow, fire fast." Do your homework on each candidate so you can make your best effort to figuratively "sit near the door."

Action Plan

When hiring candidates, do whatever you can to find out the information that is not on their resume or application.

27

HELP YOUR PLAYERS KNOW THAT
WHAT THEY DO MATTERS

MY PLAYERS ALWAYS KNEW THAT WE WERE PLAYING FOR A PURPOSE. FIGURING out a purpose, in the world of sports, is easy because a big shiny trophy is presented at the end of the competition. However, one thing I always reminded my teams was that beyond the trophy and bragging rights, they were playing for their teammates, who had worked really hard, and their parents, who had given up their summer weekends at the beach to attend softball games. And that did not even include the $350 bats, $75 gloves, gas, hotels, meals, and sometimes flights. It was important for the girls to know that they were playing for more than a big trophy and an Instagram photo.

A study that my chief human resources officer told me about regarding employee engagement claimed that 20 percent of the respondents said they love their job because they are passionate about the work, while almost 70 percent said they stay at their jobs because they feel there is a purpose. Purpose trumps passion. As a leader, it is your job to help them identify that purpose and then give them the tools to achieve it.

At our company, we make boxes. Supplying boxes does not sound very exciting or important, but it is! I like to remind my team that we do not just make boxes—we help people. Without our boxes, people could not transport food safely to supermarkets. We make boxes for snowplow parts so people can safely get to work or school in the winter. Our boxes carry critical medical supplies that save lives and sports and leisure products so we can all have fun after work. Does the box clear driveways or feed people? No, of course not. But without boxes, the world would literally shut down. This was never clearer than during the worldwide COVID-19 pandemic when every one of our employees, along with healthcare providers, first responders, and most members of the food and medical supply chain were considered essential.

Leadership guru Simon Sinek calls it "the why." What is your why? More importantly, do your leadership team and other employees understand the why of your business. Like at Volk Packaging, the purpose has to be greater than just making a product. Find your why, and you will discover a much more engaged workforce.

Action Plan

Get your leadership team together to discuss "the why" of your business and then share it with all your employees.

28

FOLLOW A PROCESS

ABBY RUTT HAD THE BEST SWING I HAD EVER SEEN. SHE WAS ONLY 14 YEARS old when she moved to my town, but I already knew who she was. She originally lived in another town over an hour away, but we had played against her several times over the previous years. As the middle school softball coach, I was thrilled when my daughter came home from the first day of eighth grade and said, "You'll never guess who moved to Scarborough! Abby Rutt!"

We already had an incredibly talented team, and now we had added one of the best young softball players in Maine to it. I could not believe my luck. We were only a couple of games into the season when I was able to capture Abby hitting a triple on my little Panasonic camera that took 30 pictures in a second. When I uploaded the pictures, I knew I was looking at something special. I pulled 10 of those photos, printed them, and used them for the rest of my coaching career to show my players what a near-perfect softball swing looked like, frame by frame. Now, I understand that different players have different styles and quirks to their swings, but there absolutely is a right way to do things, and those 10 photos of Abby's swing demonstrated that way.

When it comes to the workplace, it is critical that your company has a process for whatever you are doing. Gino Wickman writes about this at length in his book *Traction*. He states that most companies have not figured out how to create processes that are repeatable and sustainable for the long term. It took me a while to figure it out as well.

In 1996, at age 26, I started my role as sales manager for Volk Packaging. I entered my first sales meeting like a bull in a china shop. I had been a sales representative for four years, had read every sales book that I could get my hands on, and had been rather successful in my territory, so I thought I had it all figured out. I literally thought, *My sales team will be so much more successful when everyone does it the way I do it.* What I failed to understand was that having an effective process did not mean my team had to be my clones.

It took me a few sales meetings along with some time on the road with my very capable sales team to figure out that there is a difference between having a process and trying to force everyone to do things exactly the same way. You can create a process for anything, from hitting a softball to selling boxes, without turning your team into identical robots. The important thing is for everyone in your organization to understand the systems, paperwork, and steps it takes to get from point A to point B. There are "best practices" in every activity that we do as humans. You would never want to stand in the batter's box with your feet crossed just as you would not want to walk into a sales call in ripped jeans and talking with vulgarity. There is a right way to do things. We have 12 salespeople at Volk Packaging, and we have learned that they all have their own styles. That is just fine as long as the fundamentals are consistent and they are representing the company based on our core values.

At Volk Packaging, I have many different types of employees—salespeople, designers, machine operators, supervisors, and managers. They all have different styles and personalities. They all have the potential to be great. I am sure you have a similar collection of people at your company. What you need to figure out, as a leader in your organization, is how to balance each player's uniqueness alongside processes proven effective by time and trials.

Action Plan

Write down what you see as the ideal process for doing each job in your organization. Look carefully and honestly at every person and every skill set in your organization. Evaluate and determine what you can accept as someone's personal style versus what processes and systems you feel are critical to the success of your entire team.

29

SLOW DOWN THE TRAINING

ILEARNED A VALUABLE LESSON WHEN I WENT BACK TO U10 AFTER COACHING my daughter all the way to U16. When it comes to coaching, it is important to coach people at the level they are at. When I returned to coaching nine- and 10-year-old players after coaching players who were 16 and 17, it took some self-discipline to not overload them with information too fast. When I found myself back on the sidelines of a U10 field for practice, I was so tempted to teach the girls everything I had learned since my last stint as a U10 coach.

As soon as I returned to coaching the younger kids, I wanted to teach them about delayed steals and how to run to second if they were walked with a player on third, and I wanted to discuss with them the multiple bunt defenses possible depending on the situation. However, I had to force myself to slow down and teach them at their level instead of where I wanted them to be.

The exact same thing can happen with new employees. As soon as you hire an employee who does not have experience, your instinct may be to pour information into the new hire so he or she can start being productive quickly. What I realized was that the training I was giving new employees was like giving someone who is thirsty a fire hose to quench their thirst. I learned that a brand-new employee needs to learn slowly so what they heard was retainable. In my enthusiasm to teach them all about our business and the world of corrugated, I ignored the important aspect of context that adds to the training. To learn something new, the recently hired employee should understand why they are learning it. That takes time and patience.

Since I came to this conclusion, I have revamped the process completely. These days, we often begin the training with a history of the company, in-depth explanations about all the slang and buzzwords in the box business, and quite a bit of exposure to what their job will be like by spending time with veteran team members. This new plan to (respectfully) treat new employees like nine-year-old softball players leaves everyone better off and results in professionals who are much more prepared to help their coworkers and customers.

Action Plan

Work with some of your experienced and more capable employees to revamp your training program. Make sure you are maintaining a pace that allows new employees to truly absorb all they are learning.

30

THINK OF YOUR PLAYERS FIRST

WHILE THIS MAY BE HARD TO HEAR, I HAVE SOME NEWS FOR YOU: YOUR business, your customers, and your team are not about you. Simon Sinek, whom I mentioned previously, also wrote a book called *Leaders Eat Last*. The basic premise of his book is to remember that your company, the organization you are leading, or the team that you are coaching is not about you. It is about your players.

I once read a quote by a Hall of Fame baseball manager who said, "Great players make great coaches. It is never the other way around." I coached a lot of terrific softball teams. During my years coaching travel softball, my teams won 24 tournaments, two state championships, and a regional championship. Additionally, my 2007 travel team finished ninth in a national tournament. I also won Little League titles and lost only one game (on a controversial call that I still have angst about!) while coaching four years of middle school softball. As much as I would love to take credit for all those titles and victories, the hard truth remains: I never struck out a single batter or recorded even one base hit. My players did all the real work, while I had the incredible pleasure of standing in the dugout or just next to third base, watching it all unfold. Softball, or any sport, is all about the players, and if I had forgotten that and made it about me, there is no way we would have been as successful all those years.

Every year at Volk Packaging, we have a company get-together that we call the Five-Year Club Party. An employee must be with the company for at least five years before they can attend. It is considered a big step in the life of a Volk Packaging employee.

Every year at the party, we present an award that we named the Benjamin Volk Award for Excellence (BVA). My father created the award in

1995 when my grandfather, our company patriarch, was dying of cancer. He knew that September would likely be the last time my grandfather would be healthy enough to attend.

We decided that the award would be given to someone who had exemplified, over a lengthy period, the ideals that my grandfather espoused when he was CEO. The most critical was his internally famous statement that is still today our guiding principle for how we run the business: "Our customers are our bread and butter." The BVA is awarded to someone who embodies what Volk Packaging is all about. The employee must fully embody and live by our core values: customer-centricity, accountability, respect, and excellence. In addition, the BVA winner must show a love for the company and the culture that my grandfather built the company around. No one loved Volk Packaging like my grandfather did!

My father, uncle, and I all agreed that our vice president of operations, Mike Rousselle, would be the ideal first winner. Along with the honor of being named the Benjamin Volk Award winner, we present a beautiful glass sculpture to the honoree (a larger version sits in the lobby with all the winners' names etched into it), a generous monetary award, and a much-coveted parking spot for the entire length of tenure at the company.

Why do I tell this story in a chapter about thinking of your players first? Because of the parking spot.

I lose a lot of respect for owners, presidents, and CEOs who give themselves the best parking spot at their facilities. I see it at schools as well. The principal and vice principal have the parking spots closest to the door. What kind of message does that send? I love seeing all the BVA parking spot signs when pulling into Volk Packaging. It fills me with pride and joy to see the names of people who committed so much of their lives to the company with my name on it. Sometimes I arrive late and have to park at the back of the lot. I have no problem with that. Many people over the years have asked me why I don't have my own parking spot. My answer is always the same: "Why would I? I've never won the Benjamin Volk Award." And since I choose the winner, I never will. Because my employees come first.

Every day, whether you go to work, lead a non-profit, or are coaching a team, you should be asking yourself, "What can I do today to help my team be the best they can be? How can I help them succeed at whatever it is that they do? How can I make sure they know how much they matter to me, both professionally and personally?" In other words, how can I put them first?

Action Plan

Block out 10 time slots of at least 30 minutes in your calendar over the next month. Have one-on-one meetings, ideally out of the office over a meal, to ask 10 people on your team, "What can I do to help you?" And then the real challenge starts—shut up and listen.

31

MAKE A PLAN, BUT BE FLEXIBLE

FOR EVERY GAME THAT I EVER COACHED, I WENT IN WITH A PLAN, ESPECIALLY for the pitching. The game of softball is heavily dependent on pitching. I would dare say even more than in baseball. Because of that, it was critical to the success of the team to know who was pitching the upcoming game. I also had to think about who would pitch the following game and maybe even a game or two after that.

On tournament weekends, if things go well, it is not unusual to play between four and six games on a single Sunday. If you go into a day when your team might be playing as many as 42 innings, you better have a plan. Unlike baseball, softball pitchers have the ability to throw multiple games in a day. The strain on the shoulder is not at all what it is in baseball where pitchers are guided by pitch counts and then need several days' rest between games.

My daughter Lilly, at age 14, led us to a championship while pitching 32 innings on one Sunday. I had my radar gun, and she was throwing as hard at 9 p.m. as she was at 7 a.m. She could do it, but her body was tired on the ride home. Trust me, as cool as that was to watch, it was definitely not the plan my coaches and I had going into that single elimination Sunday.

We had planned, as we often did, to have two pitchers throw a combination of three innings and four innings or vice versa, depending on how the game was going. Of course, if a pitcher was throwing a no-hitter or even a shutout into the fourth inning, we had to make a tough decision. Do we pull her while she is throwing great so we can save her arm if we need it later, or do we let her finish the game while she is cruising through the competition's batters? It was often a decision the coaches and I discussed for two or three innings prior to making the final call. The game strategy always started the same. We always had a plan but were not so rigid we would not make a change to it as circumstances presented themselves.

As a leader in your business, you need a plan.

And just like when you're coaching a softball team, you also must remain flexible. You may come to work in the morning with a sure-fire plan to close a new customer or change up how you run an order. You and your leadership team may have discussed it for days and you are ready to make it happen. But then someone calls in sick or the buyer you thought you were going to be making your sales pitch to brings the CFO into the meeting without telling you. As the saying goes, "We make plans, and God laughs."

Your job as a leader is to have a toolbox full of options for dozens of possible scenarios. When you work on a project around the house, you grab your toolbox, but rarely, if ever, do you use every tool in the box. What is in your toolbox for every part of your organization's needs? Does your team know how each of those tools works so they can pull out the one they need when circumstances change?

Having the tools is only a part of this process. You must work with and train your team so that they understand how to be flexible enough to adapt when these situations arise. If your team is rigid, your customers will sense that inflexibility and will likely find a vendor more fluid. The only thing you can count on in life and business is that things will change. Nothing stays the same forever.

These are critical questions that you need to have answers to for every aspect of your business. What is your plan for 90 days, one year, three years, and so on? Make plans with the knowledge, and comfort, that it is very likely the story will not unfold exactly as you envisioned. As my favorite band, Rush, sings in their legendary song "Tom Sawyer," "Changes aren't permanent, but change is!"

Action Plan

Read the book *Traction: Get a Grip on Your Business* by Gino Wickman to learn a time-tested process for how to make plans, but always remember that the only thing that never changes is that change is inevitable.

32

LEAD THE PLAYERS AND LET THEM DO THEIR JOBS

I HAVE NEVER PUT MYSELF IN A SOFTBALL GAME THINKING I COULD STRIKE OUT THE next batter or knock in a much-needed run. Likewise, I do not have any customers that are in a territory with my name on them. I have an impressive sales team and amazing customer service representatives. I count on them to service our almost 1,000 active customers.

As leaders, we are tasked with leading people rather than doing everything ourselves. I know many business owners who manage enormous amounts of their company's customer base. What will happen when they begin to strategize for their own exit? How will they transition their company to new leadership if they are, metaphorically speaking, the chef, waiter, and dishwasher?

It is the people you lead who will take your organization where you want it to go. History can point to people like Alexander the Great and *Braveheart* legend William Wallace who actually went into battles, but for the most part, leaders lead people. It is very true that great players make great leaders. However, a great leader has the ability to take quite average people and deliver amazing results. To prove this point, just look at what George Washington did in the Revolutionary War. Those men were barely trained fighters, yet their inspiring leader helped them defeat the most powerful military force since the Roman Empire. Do not underestimate and devalue your influence as a leader. As the saying goes, "I would rather fight an army of lambs led by a lion than an army of lions led by a lamb." Whether you are a coach, the owner of a company, or leading some other kind of organization, it is best to set the vision and then lead people to drive the mission.

I am the company visionary. I set the vision for the direction of the organization, but I do not drive every aspect of that vision. I hired, trained, and count on very capable people to do their jobs. My plant manager oversees the factory, my director of sales makes sure the sales team is out hustling and bringing in new business, my CFO ensures that I get timely and accurate financial statements, my design manager monitors the sample requests to ensure we send quality prototypes to the customers and prospects, and my CHRO takes care of all the human resources issues so I am not bogged down by them. I hire good people and let them do their jobs.

Action Plan

Keep track of your tasks, every single one of them, for a week. At the end of the week, review your list to see if there's anything you can delegate so you can focus on bigger-picture activities. I did this a few years ago and concluded the day with a list of 117 tasks that someone else could do! I hired an executive assistant, and my life at work and my productivity have never been better because of it.

33

WHEN YOU GET A GOOD PITCH, SWING

I ALWAYS TOLD MY PLAYERS THAT IF YOU GET A GOOD PITCH, BE SURE TO SWING because it may be the only strike you will see. So many times, in the game of softball, the first pitch of the at-bat is the best one. In fact, for younger players or in Little League, that first pitch strike may be the only ball you even have a chance to swing at. Many U10 and U12 pitchers are new to pitching, so they throw a lot of balls. So, if you see a pitch coming in over the plate, and you want an opportunity to drive the ball, you had better take a swing at it.

In the business world, the same concept applies for sales. I have used this analogy with salespeople on many occasions. We have had situations where an opportunity arose to grab a new piece of business, and we failed to do it. We waited out of fear. When the sales representative tried later, the opportunity no longer existed.

There were times when we had a prospect sitting right on the hook, and yet, for whatever reason the sales representative did not want to set the hook and reel the customer in. It could have been that we were busy in our factory at the time, so the salesperson was worried we would miss the first delivery. It could be we had new machinery coming on, so they decided to wait to take an order after the new machinery had arrived. I could probably name another 25 reasons why a sales representative might be reluctant to swing. Whenever these cases arise, no matter what is happening at my company, I have always reminded my sales team that if the pitch comes in and they have a chance to hit it, they had better swing!

There are a multitude of reasons why you have to swing when the opportunity arises. For example, buyers with whom salespeople build great relationships move to other jobs. Companies struggle and decide to cut costs and move to the lowest price they can find (rarely Volk

Packaging). Product line changes, so the box you were working on gets eliminated from their production needs. A new chief financial officer who has a relationship with another box supplier joins the prospect's business. The local company is purchased by an out-of-state or venture capital company that has a national contract with another box company. Suffice it to say, strike while the iron is hot because who knows if that opportunity will ever come again?

There are a number of clichés I could use to explain this philosophy. I could say, like I just did, "Strike while the iron is hot," or "A bird in the hand is better than two in the bush," or even go with the ultimate cliché, "Carpe diem." But I just like to say, "Swing away!"

Action Plan

What action have you been hesitating to tackle due to fear? Stop procrastinating. Go for it!

34

MAKE A DECISION

I AM NOT SURE IF THIS IS A MYTH OR REALITY, BUT YOGI BERRA IS WIDELY REPORTED to have once said, "If you get to a fork in the road, take it." As silly as that may sound, it has some real legitimacy. One of the worst traits in a leader, whether they coach a sports team or run a business, is indecision. You will have more regrets in life because of indecision than you will ever have from failure because if you failed, that means you at least tried. Legendary Oakland A's and St. Louis Cardinals manager Tony LaRussa once said, "Being a successful manager means understanding that when everything about a decision seems right, the outcome may still end up wrong."

There were plenty of situations I had as a coach in which I was convinced that I was making the right decision. Some decisions worked out well, and some backfired on my team. I recall a game when I was pitching a certain player in a game only to watch as she gave up several runs in the first inning. It just wasn't her day. Another time, I remember creating a batting order that I was convinced made sense for the game that we were about to play only to see runners get stuck on bases because no one could knock them home. I also had times when I decided to send a girl home from third base only to have her thrown out at the plate without much of an effort by the defense. Every time this happened, the decisions seemed so obvious in the moment that I made them but did not work out as planned. Everything you know, all your past experiences, and softball coaching 101 lead you to believe that the decision you are making could only have one outcome, a good one. And then, much to your surprise, it blows up in your face. While you stand on the field, or in the dugout, shocked at the outcome, you can bet there are nine or 10 parents in the bleachers, "Monday morning quarterbacks," all speculating out loud about what you were possibly thinking.

In 2004, as my business was rapidly growing, I made the decision to buy a brand-new machine from a company with no history in the United States. We were going to be their first machine in North America. I was convinced this was a great idea because they would make sure I got exceptional customer service, as I was their North American showroom. It seemed obvious to me that they understood that if their first machine placed in an American box plant was a total bust, I would tell many of my peers and competitors. That word of mouth would be devastating to an emerging company trying to break into the United States market. Their salespeople did a fantastic job convincing me that my logic was correct, and they certainly did have an enormous interest in taking great care of our machine and my team supporting it.

Almost as soon as the new machine arrived, red flags started going up all over the place. The machine that was sold to us with the promises of cutting-edge technology and 24-hour service did not live up to any of the expectations. The machinery was poorly made, and the service we received was atrocious. I beat myself up over this decision for several years. It was a huge drain on the morale of my team who count on me to provide them with quality equipment so they can do their jobs effectively and efficiently. Every time I walked into the factory, I felt so bad for them and myself. The difference was that I was able to go back to my office and go about my day. They were stuck messing around with that horrible machine for eight hours a day! The impact that has on people is completely draining. It is very challenging to wake up excited to go to work when you know you'll spend most of the day fighting a horribly designed and poorly manufactured machine just to make a decent box. I would say things like, "This was, without a doubt, the worst decision I have ever made in my career." Friends, family, and coworkers would do their best to make me feel better with platitudes such as, "You made the best decision at the time based on what you were being told and with the information that you had available."

While I know they were trying to be kind, it failed to even slightly change how I felt. Just because you made what you thought was a good decision in the moment does not alter the fact that it was not a good decision.

I am a licensed skydiver. I know the risks, and I prepare carefully for every jump. I study the clouds and watch wind patterns. I know who else is jumping with me, and I plan my landing pattern. I could decide to jump out of a plane without taking these precautions because I've jumped so many times. It may seem like a fine decision, but when I hit the pavement or land in the trees, whatever reasons I had for thinking it was a good decision would quickly be proven incorrect. That may be an extreme analogy, but you get the point.

Although the decision to buy that machine did not work out the way I had hoped it would, the one thing I did right was that I made a decision. I did not just sit back due to fear or anxiety about making the wrong decision. My company needed new machinery, so I acted. The good news, especially in business, is that few decisions, whether good or bad, have to be permanent. In 2008, only four years later, I made another decision. I sold that machine and bought a new one that made everyone much happier and my company much more successful.

Action Plan

The next time you have an opportunity to make a decision, instead of getting sucked into paralysis by analysis, make a decision! And if you make an unwise decision, don't beat yourself up like I did for four years—make another one that improves the first one.

35

REMEMBER THE FUNDAMENTALS

ALL OF FAME BASEBALL LEGEND CAL RIPKIN JR. SAID, "DO THE LITTLE THINGS right, and the big things take care of themselves." We all enjoy learning unique and interesting tactics and strategies in sports and in life. During my years as a softball coach, especially under the tutelage of coach Tom Griffin, I learned many cool tricks of the sport. I learned subtle things that could be done to make our team better and to win more games. I would never take away the advantages that my teams had by learning and, more importantly, executing those outside-the-box strategies. However, the most effective tactic you can possibly have in any sport or activity is the skill of mastering the fundamentals.

Stealing home, fake bunts, and trick plays are all helpful ways to gain a little advantage. Creative strategies and tactics are sometimes needed to win a softball game. But none of those mean a thing if you can't hit, catch, and throw extremely effectively. Your team having the ability to pull off a trick play will not help you if the next time your team is in the field, your players drop an easy pop fly and make wild throws. Learning how to effectively carry out a double steal is a completely useless skillset if nobody on your team can hit the ball in order to get your players on the bases to begin with.

I do not know much about your business, and I do not need to know much about your business. The one thing I do absolutely know about your business, regardless of whether you are making boxes or widgets, selling a service, or running a nonprofit, is that I guarantee there are fundamentals that are critical to your company's success. There are fundamentals not only in your role as a leader but also within every part of your business. My sales team's fundamentals require them to be fearless in talking to strangers and understanding price objections. My production crews must know the basics of how to run the machinery. The design department needs math skills and the ability to visualize three-dimensionally. My human resources team cannot do their jobs without a high degree of emotional intelligence. As I said, every person who reads this book will have a different set of fundamentals that are important to their job and their success. But make no mistake, the fundamentals do exist. There are no exceptions.

As mentioned above, at Volk Packaging, we have fundamentals that differ by department and even machine to machine, but we also share some fundamentals across the company: We all focus on taking care of the customer first.

We must respect each other.

We must make good boxes.

We cannot be so high priced that nobody wants to buy from us.

We have no choice but to pay close attention to our costs.

These are just some of the fundamentals that keep our business going. What are your fundamentals? Work on them always. And make sure everybody else is doing so too.

Action Plan

Determine the fundamentals of each department in your company and assess whether your team has a firm grasp of them. Prevent your company from dying by proactively training your employees in the fundamentals of the company and their department.

36

SOMETIMES IT'S BEST TO STICK YOUR SUPERSTAR IN RIGHT FIELD

IT WAS MY FIRST YEAR COACHING LITTLE LEAGUE. WE WERE PLAYING IN THE second or third game of the season without our best player. I had no idea where she was. I just knew she wasn't at our game, so I was making do with the players that I had. In the bottom of the third inning (I can't remember if we were winning or losing), my star player showed up for the game. When I asked her where she was, she told me that she had just finished a travel soccer game.

I had no problem with girls playing multiple sports. In fact, throughout my entire coaching career, I encouraged it. I believe travel sports, as much as I enjoyed them, have done a disservice to kids by pushing them to be one-sport athletes. All research and almost every study will tell you that kids are better off playing multiple sports. If you look at the life of almost any professional athlete, you will find that they were multi-sport athletes early in their lives. Playing more than one sport has many advantages, beginning with preventing burnout of young athletes.

My only stipulation regarding my players participating in multiple sports was that when softball season started, the softball team was their top priority. If we had a softball game in the fall and a girl had a soccer game, I would tell her to go to the soccer game. If we had a practice in January and my player had a basketball game, I would tell her to go play basketball. But when April arrived and those sports are not in season and softball was, I expected them to be at practice and games over their other sports commitments. So, when my 12-year-old superstar showed up in the middle of the game, I told her to go play right field. She looked at me and said, "I don't play outfield."

I simply smiled and said, "You do when you show up in the third inning.

In Chapter 22, I wrote about how team players do not have to be treated the same to be treated fairly. That principle does not apply to this scenario. It is one thing to treat a 20-year employee differently than a six-month employee, but it is another to allow a star player to take advantage of their value to the team or the company. As a leader, it is important to know which rules are bendable and which rules are not. The employee who has been with you for 20 years and needs to take a day off for a personal issue may be treated differently than someone who has been with you for six months and wants the day off for a personal issue. The 20-year veteran has earned some flexibility. But while that flexibility applies in some scenarios, the 20-year employee still cannot show up an hour and a half late for work.

We had a customer service representative who would meander into the office 10, 15, maybe even 20 minutes late for work. And she didn't do it once in a while—she did it on a regular basis. The issue was complex because she had an incredible relationship with our biggest customer, and we were a much smaller company at the time, so the thought of losing that huge customer was terrifying. However, the tardy employee was not being fair to the company, her coworkers, or to me. We talked with her. We tried to work with her. We practically begged her to show up to work on time. But she was a star with this customer, so she thought she could make her own rules under the false assumption that she was untouchable. Finally, we made the difficult decision to terminate her employment and risked losing our biggest customer. It was an agonizing decision, fraught with potential downside. However, once we fired her and retained the customer, morale in the department went through the roof. Even though it might be a hard decision, sticking your star player in right field can bring positive results and improve the morale of the team as a whole.

Action Plan

Look around your company. Talk to your managers and supervisors. If you have a star player showing up in the third inning, stick her in right field!

37

AN ACCURATE THROW LATE IS BETTER THAN A WILD THROW ON TIME

WHEN I WAS COACHING SOFTBALL, I ALWAYS TOLD MY PLAYERS THAT I would rather see them make an accurate throw a little late than make a rushed throw that could be wild. I would be much happier seeing the player plant her feet and throw it right to the first baseman than just hurling the ball willy-nilly, hoping it gets to first.

If a shortstop makes a wild throw to first base, an out could still be made if the first baseman manages to snag the bad throw. But it's just as likely that the ball sails by the first baseman and could potentially bounce off the fence or the dugout, ricochet into right field, and all of a sudden, the runner is not only safe at first base but potentially on second base or even third base. If they make a wild throw from the outfield, instead of the ball going to the second baseman, it could fly past the second baseman, and who knows where it could end up or where the runner might stop. Accuracy is more important than speed.

Interestingly, this is a major problem with our media today. With 24-hour news and online news, many reporters are much more interested in getting the story out quickly than getting it out accurately. In the last 10 years, I have had several negative experiences, particularly with newspapers, writing a story about my company or me. It has been very frustrating to see these stories contain inaccuracies and misinformation. All they had to do was take a little extra time to send me the story before publishing it so I could confirm whether or not the information was correct. For example, when my company was named Maine's Family Business of the Year, the article in the local newspaper called me Dexter throughout the entire story.

I use the analogy of a rushed throw from shortstop frequently at my company. It is more important to make quality boxes, to get a customer the right information, and to do paperwork correctly than to do any of those things quickly. Accuracy should always trump expediency. There is an old cliché in business that says, "You can have it cheap. You can have it right. You can have it quickly. Choose two." If a customer wants something good and right, it is going to cost a little more. If a customer wants something cheap and fast, it is unlikely to be very good. And if a customer would like their order cheap and right, it may take a bit extra time. At Volk Packaging, we are rarely the lowest-priced box option in the market, and I am fine with that, so we work twice as hard to provide our customers with products that are right and arrive quickly. Of course, my company and most businesses try for all three, but like a softball player with three at-bats in a game, it is very difficult to go three for three on a consistent basis.

Action Plan

Meet with your team to define what is most important at your company and with your customers. I definitely think getting it right is more important than doing it fast. Pull some recent orders and discuss with your crews if you were focused on right over fast.

38

FIGHT FOR YOUR PLAYERS

SHORTLY AFTER I WAS HIRED TO COACH THE LOCAL MIDDLE SCHOOL SOFTBALL team for the second time, school administrators sat me down to explain my roster situation. When this meeting occurred, I had already had several practices, and I had a good sense of the players on the team, both good and bad. One of the aspects of coaching middle school that I took great pleasure in was the fact that I had girls on the team who had been playing travel ball since they were nine years old and girls on the team who had literally never picked up a softball bat or glove in their life. I loved the mix of playing skills and the fun that they had together.

The middle school athletic director told me that I had to cut two girls because the baseball team had been cut to 16 boys, but I had 18 girls. There were about 50 boys who tried out for the baseball team, but only 18 girls came out for softball tryouts. It would have been very easy for me to pick which girls were not going to make the team because I had one girl on the team who had never played before and another girl with special needs. I knew that for those two girls, this was going to be their one and only experience playing a team sport. There was no chance that either of them would even play junior varsity when they got to high school because the town I was coaching in was a softball powerhouse. Not even average players made the high school team. Players that would have been four-year varsity softball players in other towns would be cut in our town.

I looked the athletic director right in the eyes, and I said, "Sorry. There is no way I'm cutting anyone. If you want to cut players, you can find a new coach. This is the one chance that some of these girls have to play a competitive sport, and I'm not going to take it away from them. Someday, God willing, these girls will become parents. And when their daughter is in middle school, and they suggest playing softball, I want those moms to be able to tell their daughters, 'I played softball when I was in school.'"

I even pictured those kids looking at their mom and saying, "What?! You played softball?"

I had no idea whether that conversation would ever happen for them, but I was not going to be the one to prevent the possibility. Fortunately, and this may shock you, there are not a ton of people lining up for the job of middle school softball coach. I knew I was negotiating from a position of strength. Regardless of your level of power, sometimes it is necessary to fight for your players. The athletic director relented, so our team had 18 players as planned.

In the business world, a version of this scenario happens on a regular basis. As the leader, you are the one everyone looks at to determine their value in the organization. Yes, they have supervisors, managers, and other people that they report to. However, at the end of the day, you have the ability to make them feel valued and special, and you have the power to make them feel unvalued and unappreciated. There are a lot of ways that you can make your employees feel like they matter. Few of those will mean more to them than seeing you fight on their behalf.

We had a customer who was, to put it gently, a jerk! He was rude to the point where he would even swear at my sales representative in person and yell at my customer service staff over the phone. I was unaware of this situation for a couple of years. One day, my salesman called me because the customer had just ripped into him in a tirade of curse words and insults. I have absolutely no patience for that kind of disrespect towards anyone at my company. It is completely unacceptable, so I told the salesman it was time to fire this customer. Of course, he did not want to do that. The purchaser bought a decent amount of product, and he did not want to lose the account. He was worried about making his sales quota without this customer and, not wanting a hostile confrontation, was also very apprehensive about ending business with a long-time customer because of how he might react.

I did not hesitate when I said, "Give me his number, and I'll call him. He fires off one dirty word to me, and I will be happy to fire him."

I also assured the salesman that I would reduce his quota by the customer's sales so it would not affect his pay. I was not going to stand by, knowing that one of my loyal employees, someone I considered a friend, was being mistreated. He was still hesitant to share the phone number.

Again, I said, "Please give me the number. I'll call him right now." I added, "This isn't just about you. How he treats you and others at Volk Packaging is a reflection on me. So, not only is it unacceptable that he is verbally abusing you, as far as I'm concerned, if I allow it, then I am an accomplice to that abuse."

He reluctantly gave me the jerk's number. It only took about three minutes before he threw an f-bomb at me. Remaining calm and composed, I said, "Sir, I think it's time that you find another supplier because we are not going to sell you boxes anymore. You are obviously dissatisfied with our service, so we are going to free you to go elsewhere."

He screamed, "Fine!" And then he hung up the phone. In actuality, he probably slammed down the phone. I have to be honest—it felt really good to fire this guy. My sales representative, although still uncomfortable with the whole situation, tells me to this day how much he appreciated that I made the phone call. Just like with those two girls who were going to be cut, I fought for my player. Did this impact the morale of the rest of the company? Not at all. I doubt more than a few people even knew that I did this. Fighting for your players is not an action that you do because it builds morale or sends a message to the rest of the employees. It is usually a person-by-person, situation-by-situation activity that, over time, creates an environment in which your employees know you have their backs. But once you do it a few times, word gets around.

Action Plan

Find two or three employees (maybe more if you have a large company) who are dealing with something difficult and fight for them. You will not only gain their loyalty, but that action will also slowly and inevitably ripple through your company faster than you can believe, creating loyalty, respect, and appreciation.

39

YOU DON'T WANT TO REMEMBER THE UMPIRE

WHEN YOU COACH A SOFTBALL GAME, YOU DO NOT WANT TO REMEMBER THE umpire later in the day. If the umpire does a good job, no one can even remember what he or she looked like. In fact, only when the umpire screws up a call or does something to anger you can you even tell anyone what he looked like after the game. If the umpire calls balls as strikes and strikes as balls, trust me, you remember exactly what he looked like.

I like to use the umpire scenario as an analogy when talking with my customers, especially my potential customers who are not familiar with us as a vendor. Remembering umpires is very similar to box suppliers because no one wakes up in the morning hoping to be thinking about their boxes all day. They want to make their own product and work on being successful. It is only when the box supplier sends in bad product, has a late delivery, or does not respond to someone's needs that the customer starts thinking about their boxes. I explain to my customers that we want to be like the good umpire. I say to them, "We don't want you worrying or even thinking about boxes during your workday. Let us do that."

When I was 24 years old and selling in central Maine, I had the privilege of taking my 84-year-old grandfather out on the road with me to visit customers. He was the founder of the company and an amazing salesman going all the way back to the 1930s. We visited a customer who split her box business between Volk Packaging and another supplier. We had a nice visit, but when we got back to the car, my grandfather felt I was missing a perfect opportunity with this customer. He said, "You should do their inventory!"

I said, "What do you mean?

He said, "They have two suppliers. The buyer clearly likes working with you. If you want her to give you all the business, you should tell her that all she has to do is tell you how many boxes they want on their floor. You will go in twice a week and do a physical inventory count. If they need more boxes, you will arrange it and deliver them a couple of days later. Make her life easier. Take the buying of boxes right off her desk, and she'll give you 100 percent of her business."

A few days later, I gave her the exact speech that my grandfather recommended, and within a couple of months, I was their sole supplier. She has moved on personally, but to this day, that company has never bought a box from anyone other than Volk Packaging. Why would they? We became an awesome "umpire."

Action Plan

Be a good umpire. Talk to your team about what you can do to make the lives of your customers easier so that they like you but are not thinking about you too much.

40

PLAY UP

NOTHING IS WORSE TO A U14 TEAM MADE UP OF 13- AND 14-YEAR-OLDS THAN losing to a 12-and-under team. And nothing is cooler to a U12 team made of up 11- and 12-year-old girls than beating a group of 13- and 14-year-olds.

The 13- and 14-year-olds cannot think of anything worse than losing to a 12-and-under team. The 12-and-under team would be absolutely ecstatic if they could beat a group of 13- and 14-year-old girls. That is why when I coached a team, we would play up before the season started whenever possible. The girls would often get very worried when we played an older team. They were worried about getting hit by the ball. They were worried about being embarrassed. And because most of these girls were very competitive, they were concerned about losing. Before the "play up" games began, I would point out that we had nothing to lose. The pressure was all on the older girls. If we were to lose the game, nobody would think anything of it. Everyone would just say to themselves, "Sure, they lost. They're younger." This made perfect sense to the younger girls and took a lot of pressure off them. In fact, it ended up making them excited to play up instead of anxious. If we were to beat the older girls, that would be huge. Everyone expects the older team to win, and they expect us to lose, so how could the pressure be on anybody but the older players?

I used the same thought process when I was coaching the middle school softball team. From very early in the season, I started pestering the baseball coach about having a scrimmage. He justifiably did not want to play us for the same reasons I just mentioned. Why would he? He had everything to lose and very little to gain. If his boys won, so what? They beat a bunch of girls. But, oh my, if they lost?!

One of the years I coached middle school, we were on the bus on our way back from the sixth game of the season. The baseball coach came over to me and said, "Do you still want to scrimmage the boys?"

I didn't hesitate. "Heck yeah, we do!"

The baseball coach said, "Okay, let's do it."

I asked him what changed his mind. In all my years coaching middle school softball, no baseball coach ever agreed to a scrimmage against my girls. His response still cracks me up. He said, "These boys need a little wake-up call. They are not nearly as good as they think they are, and they need to be shown that. And the best way to show them would be to lose to the girls. So, I hope you kick our butts."

A few days later, that is exactly what we did! We played four or five innings after our practices that day. My daughter Lilly started the game, and another pitcher finished it. Lilly faced nine boys. She struck out five of them, and the other four hit weak infield ground balls. Not a single boy got on base. My other pitcher faired about the same. The boys walked away without the same cocky attitude that was driving their coach nuts. It was mission accomplished for both coaches.

My relatively small box company with one location in Southern Maine must play up almost every day. We compete against privately held companies that are much bigger and have deeper pockets than we do, and we compete against Fortune 100 companies whose pockets are even deeper. Like when a U12 team plays up against a U14 team, we do not win every one of the battles. My team does an amazing job competing against the behemoth competitors that want our customers. Sometimes we simply get outgunned. As frustrating as that may be for my sales team, and for me, I would rather lose by playing up than win all the time by playing down.

Action Plan

Do you have a competitor that you are afraid to compete against? Is there a market that you do not think you can win business in? Ignore those fears! Figure out what it is about your business that separates you from the big players in your region. Do you have better service? Is it because you are locally owned? Do you give back to the community in ways your competitor doesn't? Is there something about your product line that distinguishes itself as more advantageous to the customer?

There are as many ways you can distinguish yourself from the bigger competitors as there will be people reading this book. In the incredible story of David and Goliath, David realized that his advantage was that God was on his side. He calmly picked up five smooth stones and took down a giant. I cannot tell you what makes your company a David versus a Goliath. But I can tell you that you will be better off if you are not afraid to pick up some smooth stones and play up.

41

BE PREPARED TO BE DISLIKED

THE MOST COMMON REALITY OF ALL COACHES AND BOSSES IS ONE THING—WE must be prepared to be disliked. Whether you are coaching a Little League team, a high school team, or a major league team, some people are not going to like your decisions, and therefore, they are not going to like you! I have experienced this many times during my years as a coach and a boss.

I was coaching a Little League semifinal game in which I left my number one pitcher in for the whole game. Following the game, I was confronted, very angrily, in the parking lot by my number two pitcher's family. They could not understand why I left our top pitcher in for the whole game. The fact that it was a 1–0 game that would take us to the championship and that my number two pitcher was significantly worse than my number one pitcher did not matter. All that mattered to her family was that she didn't get to pitch.

I also remember a call from an upset father after a pre-season scrimmage game. We had not even started the actual season when I received a very hostile phone call from him. He asked why his daughter had not played infield in the scrimmage game. She was a decent hitter, but she could not catch a line drive because she was, unfortunately, afraid of the ball. I tried to explain to the father that I could not place his daughter in the infield until I was comfortable that she could protect herself if a line drive was hit straight at her. I was concerned about her safety more than her playing position preference. Somehow, he seemed completely oblivious to his daughter's obvious fielding challenges. He not only took his daughter off my team, but he also spent the entire summer bad-mouthing me to anyone that would listen. As a coach, you had better be prepared for people not to like you.

Any business owner, manager, or supervisor will experience remarkably similar criticisms, second-guessing, and unrealistic expectations. No matter what you do or how well you do it, someone is not going to like you. Sometimes they will have a legitimate issue with you. You cannot make great decisions every time. But even when you do make great decisions, people will still have gripes about you.

I cannot honestly tell you that I have ever fully accepted the cold, hard fact that leadership inevitably alienates some people. I don't think too many people enjoy it when someone dislikes or disrespects them or badmouths them behind their back. When you are in a situation like I am, with over 100 employees, it is virtually guaranteed that someone will be unhappy with you on a regular basis, maybe even daily. It is not going to happen just occasionally. I would be willing to bet that at any given moment of any given year in the 30 years I have been running my company, there has hardly been a minute in which there was not somebody who thought I sucked. Every year at our company Christmas party, I literally give thousands of dollars away using a roulette wheel that my employees spin for cash prizes. That day, I am pretty popular. However, a week later, when the Christmas bonuses come out, it is almost a sure thing that there will be a handful of people who feel like they deserve a lot more. They open their Christmas bonus envelope, and bam, my popularity from the week prior disappears instantly.

You can try to weed out anyone on your team or in your business who does not care for you, but you will be basically chasing your tail. As soon as you cut the player who does not like you or fire the employee who believes with all his heart that the company would be better off without you, there will be somebody else right behind that person who has the same opinion. When you are a coach, or a boss, having someone dislike you is like death and taxes—unavoidable.

I wish I could tell you how to solve this problem, but I do not have any sage advice. If you cannot be comfortable understanding that as a coach or a boss, you will pretty much always have somebody who thinks you are underestimating their ability, underpaying them, or not doing a good job, then coaching or leading an organization may not be your calling. You may not like being disliked but, as a leader, get prepared for it. And believe it or not, if you can hang in there and not give up, after a while you kind of get used to it so it doesn't even bother you that much.

Action Plan

Be kind to your spouse, take good care of your kids, and call your mom. If they like you, it will be a lot easier to accept when your player or employee does not. And never let the haters get you down.

42

HAVE THE TOUGH CONVERSATIONS, EVEN WHEN YOU REALLY DON'T WANT TO

I AM A MIDDLE CHILD WHO GREW UP IN A HOUSE WITH VERY LITTLE CONFLICT. I DO not like conflict. In fact, I hate it, but I cannot avoid it. Sometimes you must have difficult conversations. People in the workplace do not like to be confronted with things they don't want to hear, but it is part of what you signed up for as a leader. Telling someone they are not performing well at work is upsetting to them. Telling a parent that their kid is not performing well is an entirely different animal. No one wants to hear something about their child that is not glowing, even if it is true.

I have had to initiate some very uncomfortable conversations, including firing people that I genuinely liked. These conversations are never easy, but if you can maintain your cool and be respectful, they will be a more positive experience. One particularly agonizing discussion that I had to face head-on was with a young salesman who I really cared about and personally tried to mentor. He was a really decent young man that I had great hopes for, but he was simply not ready to be a successful salesman and maybe never would be. Sales skills or not, I discovered that he had not been working. Many of his biggest customers didn't even know his name! When employees do not work but take my paycheck, I consider that stealing from my company. I have an agreement with all my employees that is very clear. They work, and I pay them. It is not complicated. To make it even worse, his dad was a good friend of mine. I sat him down to fire him with both disappointment and discouragement. There was very little part of me that wanted to be in that room for that conversation. However, when I accepted the role as a leader within my organization, I knew this was one of the responsibilities. It was a tough meeting, as expected, but we left on good terms, and I am still friendly with him today.

It took me many years to reach the point that tough conversations didn't make me feel ill. Some of that growth came from simple maturity. Some of it arose from being forced into difficult conversations, as I wanted to show my leadership skills to my father and uncle. Great leaders don't avoid hard conversations, and I have always strived to be a great leader.

Action Plan

Do you have a difficult conversation that you have been avoiding? Face it head-on. If you do it with respect for the person on the other side of the meeting, it won't be nearly as bad as you're anticipating.

43

PRAISE INTENTIONALLY AND SINCERELY

IT IS IMPORTANT TO PRAISE THE PEOPLE WHO WORK FOR YOU, OR PLAY FOR YOU, but it has to be genuine and limited. Throughout my coaching career, I worked with many assistant coaches. Some were good and really knew the game, and some were just parents willing to step up and help out as best as they could. I appreciated all of them because I knew how big a commitment it was to be my assistant coach. No different from how I work as CEO of Volk Packaging, I gave everything I had to my teams, and I expected my coaching staff to do the same. During one of my stints as a U10 coach, I had a wonderful woman who was one of my assistants. She only had a basic understanding of the game but had more enthusiasm than could be measured. She knew enough to not tell the players something unless she knew it was right. She was definitely the most positive, upbeat, and encouraging coach I had ever worked with. Interestingly, those same assets became an issue for me as the season progressed.

Everything the assistant coach said was affirming. She had a very hard time honestly critiquing a player's performance. She praised the girls for literally everything they did, even if it was not praiseworthy. If our shortstop caught a routine pop fly, she would yell, "Great catch!" If a player hit a bloop single over the pitcher's head, which allowed the batter to make it to first base, the player would arrive to hear, "Awesome hit!" Please don't get me wrong. I loved her positive vibes. What became an issue was when the players started to think that everything they did was fantastic. Even after a girl struck out looking (not swinging but watching a third strike go into the catcher's glove), she would hear, "No problem. Good at-bat!" The fact is that it was not a good at-bat. She struck out without even swinging. And catching an easy pop up or getting a single on a weak little blooper was also not praiseworthy. When you heap praise on your players for things that are just expected as part of the job or are tasks that are not actually done well, you create confusion and lower the bar of expectations.

I read one time that millennials expect seven compliments per day. I am not sure where that data originated from, but can you imagine having to find seven compliments per day for every person who works for you or is on your team? I have 110 employees. For me to meet that expectation, I would have to come up with 770 compliments per day. There are 251 workdays in a typical year at Volk Packaging which means to meet this ridiculous expectation, I would need to fork up over 193,000 compliments per year! I would spend all my days walking around, saying, "Good job, Dave," and "Excellent work, Mary!" It would be exhausting. And let's be honest. Would anyone feel that I truly appreciate them if they hear me handing out 770 compliments every day? I do not think so.

For example, I will often send a group email (cc'ing the whole leadership team) to tell a customer service representative that she did a great job when I receive a compliment from a customer praising something that happened which was perfectly handled. How would that employee feel if I also sent an email for a routine call that I overheard, praising how amazing they did? The true compliment would completely lose its power. Imagine me saying, "Hey, Mary, awesome job on that call. The customer called to ask when his order was being delivered, and you said Tuesday. WOW! I'm so impressed!" It sounds so ridiculous that she would assume I am being sarcastic or patronizing.

It is very important for your team to know that you value them, so offer praise intentionally and sincerely. Make sure that the praise is merited and the person on the other end of it realizes they did something well. If you compliment every single thing people do, whether it was actually praiseworthy or not, how will they know when you really appreciate something they did? How will they know what a truly exceptional performance is and what it is not?

Action Plan

Pick a number of compliments to give out each day that you feel are justified for the size of your team. Try to find people doing exceptional work and genuinely praise them. If you go over the number some days, terrific, and if you fall short some days because you don't want to issue unworthy praise, that is just fine, too. Either way, get in the habit of daily offering praise to show sincere appreciation, not just for the sake of doing it.

44

FINISH THE PLAY

THERE WERE TWO OUTS IN THE LAST INNING OF A U10 GAME THAT I WAS COACHING in Lowell, Massachusetts. We were up by one run, and the other team had a girl on first base. I had my best pitcher and my best catcher in the game, so I was feeling confident. There were two strikes. My pitcher threw a terrific changeup (a relatively slow pitch that has the same pitching motion as a fastball, so it messes with the batter's timing) that floated in and dropped right at the plate, exactly what it was supposed to do. The batter swung and missed. My catcher scooped the ball cleanly and then rolled it back to the pitcher's circle. Game over!

Ah, not so fast.

The umpire thought the ball hit the ground which would have made it a dropped third strike. A pitch that touches the ground before the catcher's glove is considered a dropped ball, a ball the catcher didn't catch cleanly in her glove. On a dropped third strike, the batter can run to first base. She is not out on a strikeout as would normally be the case when the umpire calls strike three. She is only out when the ball is then thrown to first base before she arrives or someone tags her with the ball.

While my players were celebrating and coming off the field, the opposing coach noticed that the umpire never called the batter out. He told his girls to start running. The player at first base and the batter began running the bases. By the time we looked up to see what was happening, they had both crossed home plate. Now the game was over for sure, but with a different winner!

I tried to argue with the umpire that my catcher had caught the ball before it hit the ground, but because it was midsummer and very dusty, he had seen a cloud of dust and assumed the ball had hit the ground. It was a bad call, but I was not getting anywhere convincing him otherwise. My team had not finished the play, and we lost the game. It was a valuable lesson learned the hard way.

The play is not over until the umpire says it is. What does that mean in the marketplace? Your business is not over until the final out, until the last dollar is spent. The sale is not dead ever. If you are breathing and the customer is buying the products that your company sells, keep working.

We had a salesman spend 22 years making sales calls to the same customer, the same buyer, without receiving a single order. He never gave up because the play was not over. He would call the buyer every six months just to say hello, biding his time and hoping their box supplier would eventually stub their toe. He knew that day might never come, but that did not stop him or even slow him down from pursuing the business. After 22 long years of persistent patience, their vendor finally dropped the ball. My salesman was the first person they thought of calling. Not only did he get an order, but it wasn't long before he was awarded all their business. We still have all their business today because he finished the play.

This is the final chapter of my book, so I have some parting advice to help you finish the play strong.

Read this book more than once.

Highlight the parts you like or want to implement.

Buy a copy for your whole leadership team. I realize this is self-serving, but you'll want everyone rowing the same direction so you all can live the principles presented in the different chapters.

Set a goal to complete at least half the Action Plans within the next year.

Read other business books. Read as many books as you can. Never ever quit learning. You can always get better.

Action Plan

Are there any initiatives in your company that your team started but did not finish? Find out why and, if any of the initiatives make sense, encourage your team to finish the play.

CONCLUSION

I **HAVE STRUGGLED WITH HOW TO CONCLUDE THIS BOOK. PART OF THE CHALLENGE** that I have had is because my brain continues to come up with more chapters. Just when I think I have said all I need to say, I think of another good lesson that I could share from either my coaching or business experiences. At some point, I just had to accept that I have said what I need to say, and the rest, if I ever want to share them, could be in a sequel. Maybe I will call it *Go for Home!*

I have enjoyed sharing my tips for coaching and running a business with you. I hope that you found some of them helpful in a meaningful way. This book should be just one step in a lifetime of learning for you. There is always another opinion, another lesson, and another perspective. I was not a great student in my school days, but since graduating college, I have always considered myself a lifelong learner. Because I'm a big fan of the band Rush, Neil Peart has been an inspiration to me. Despite being well regarded as one of the greatest drummers in all of rock n' roll, he continued to take lessons until he was tragically diagnosed with brain cancer. If a legend like Neil Peart can still learn to improve his craft well into his remarkably successful career, who am I to think that I cannot become a better leader at every stage of my life? My wish is that you have that same desire and that this book will be one you can recommend to others wanting to improve.

May the lessons in this book, and in your own experiences, give you the courage to always go for third!

APPENDIX

"BREAKING BREAD WITH DEREK" FORM

As we look forward to 2023, I'd like to ensure that we're harnessing the talent of our most important resource—you! Over the course of 2023, I will sit down and "break bread" with each member of the Volk Packaging team that I didn't meet with in the past to ask for your input. If you would like to have a second meal with me, please feel free to fill out a new form, but I will target the ones I have not done yet first.

No amount of boxes built or sold is more important than the relationships we build while working together here at VPC, and that is why I genuinely want to hear from you. The good, the bad, and the ugly, it all matters to me and the progress at Volk Packaging.

In order to best prepare to have a productive discussion, I ask that you answer the three questions enclosed in this letter and then put them in the box in the lunchroom.

Please know your privacy is important, and I want your honest opinions. Therefore, answers will only be viewed by me and only discussed between the associate and me unless otherwise agreed upon during our meeting.

If are uncomfortable meeting with me one-on-one and you and one other Volk Packaging or Volk Paxit team member would like to have a combined meeting, please list that person's name on the last page.

Please do not hesitate to reach out with any questions.

I look forward to meeting with you in **2023**.

Sincerely,

Derek S. Volk
President

What I'd like to discuss with you:

NAME: _____

What is going very well at VPC that I should know about but might not? (e.g., "Jim is the most improved member on my team in 2018," "Lisa has probably saved us thousands of dollars by changing glue suppliers," or "Dave's team is the most effective team on the floor.")

_____

_____

_____

_____

_____

What is not going very well at VPC that I should know about but might not? (e.g., "The XYZ machine is well behind its maintenance schedule," "A coworker has a habit that scares me," or "We really need to update the contact phone numbers on our website.")

_____

_____

_____

_____

What would you like me to know about you personally that I might not already know? (e.g., "My daughter is getting married in March," "My son graduates from college this spring," or "We have a family issue I think you should know about.")

_____

_____

_____

_____

_____

ABOUT THE AUTHOR

Derek Volk is the owner of Volk Packaging Corporation, a third-generation family-owned-and-operated corrugated box manufacturer, and Volk Paxit, a contract packaging fulfillment center. Derek is a philanthropist, successful businessman, former radio personality, best-selling author (www.chasingtherabbit.org), and nationally recognized public speaker. His company has won many awards under his leadership. Derek was recognized by MaineBiz as one of Maine's business trailblazers. In 2020, Derek was inducted into Maine's "Manufacturer's Hall of Fame." His opinion has repeatedly been sought by national experts, including the *Wall Street Journal*. For their support for autism issues, Derek and his family were named 2015 "Humanitarians of the Year." To learn more about Volk Packaging, visit www.volkboxes.com. And be sure to follow Volk Packaging on Facebook and connect with Derek on Facebook, Instagram, and/or LinkedIn. Derek has four children and two grandchildren.

Made in the USA
Middletown, DE
06 September 2025